Higher Functioning Adolescents and Young Adults with Autism

Higher Functioning Adolescents and Young Adults with Autism

A Teacher's Guide

Ann Fullerton
Joyce Stratton
Phyllis Coyne
Carol Gray

Illustrations by

Georgianne Thomas

8700 Shoal Creek Boulevard
Austin, Texas 78757-6897
800/897-3202 Fax 800/397-7633
Order online at http://www.proedinc.com

© 1996 by PRO-ED, Inc.
8700 Shoal Creek Boulevard
Austin, Texas 78757-6897
800/897-3202 Fax 800/397-7633
Order online at http://www.proedinc.com

Library of Congress Cataloging–in–Publication Data

Higher functioning adolescents and young adults with autism : a
    teacher's guide / [written by] Ann Fullerton . . . [et al.] :
    Georgianne Thomas, illustrator : Ann Fullerton, editor.
        p.   cm.
    Includes bibliographical references and index.
    ISBN 0-89079-681-5 (pbk. : alk. paper)
        1. Autistic youth—Education—United States.   2. Autism—United
    States.   I. Fullerton, Ann.
LC4718.H54   1996
371.94'0973—dc20   95–49439
                                                       CIP

Printed in the United States of America

5   6   7   8   9   10   07   06   05   04   03   02

To the persons with autism
who have been participant evaluators in this project
and have shared their journeys
toward self-determination.

One participant evaluator,
when asked, "What does self-determination mean to you?"
replied, "It means putting feet on my dreams."

Contents

Chapter Summaries

CHAPTER 1: WHO ARE HIGHER FUNCTIONING YOUNG ADULTS WITH AUTISM?

Author: Ann Fullerton
Department of Special & Counselor Education,
School of Education, Portland State University,
Portland, Oregon

This chapter provides the current definition of higher functioning autism and describes the sensory, cognitive, and social experiences of higher functioning persons with autism. It also gives general background information for teachers.

CHAPTER 2: ADOLESCENCE AND YOUNG ADULTHOOD

Author: Ann Fullerton

Chapter 2 explores the impact of adolescence on the person with autism. It discusses the young adult's changing relationship with peers and the process of forming an identity. This second chapter builds on the first by looking at what both students with autism and their high school peers are experiencing.

CHAPTER 3: ADAPTING INSTRUCTIONAL MATERIALS AND STRATEGIES

Author: Joyce Stratton
State Specialist, Oregon Department of Education
Statewide Autism Services, Albany, Oregon

With instructional adaptations and assistance, higher functioning students with autism can experience great success in the academic classroom. This chapter provides strategies for assessing needs and for providing the levels and types of assistance needed.

CHAPTER 4: ORGANIZATIONAL AND TIME MANAGEMENT STRATEGIES

Author: Phyllis Coyne
Autism Specialist, Columbia Regional Program Autism Services,
Portland, Oregon

Persons with autism can have difficulty sequencing, organizing, and using time concepts in their daily lives. This chapter describes a variety of organizational and time management strategies.

CHAPTER 5:   SOCIAL ASSISTANCE

Author: Carol Gray
         Consultant to Children & Adults with
              Autism,
         Jenison Public School, Jenison,
              Michigan

Persons with autism are often misunderstood by others in social situations. At the same time, they may not understand aspects of the social context and social cues present. This chapter presents specific strategies for gaining mutual understanding and for providing social assistance to persons with autism.

RESOURCES

This section is a list of resources for higher functioning persons with autism and their families, teachers, and friends.

Foreword

In the past 15 years, there has been an explosion of useful information and strategies to help parents and teachers work more effectively with children and young adults with autism. Those who are working in the field of autism have realized that some people may experience very mild or subtle autism. Consequently, they have developed effective techniques to help children and young adults labeled high functioning autistic or Asberger syndrome to realize their potential for living independent adult lives. An excellent example of these materials is *Higher Functioning Adolescents and Young Adults with Autism: A Teacher's Guide.* Our son and his high school teachers are currently using these strategies, and the results have been excellent.

We were concerned, because of Peter's easy and gentle personality, that his learning problems might not be recognized. Outwardly, he seems to be the "perfect" student. He follows rules conscientiously and is so quiet that we were afraid that if we didn't meet with the teachers fairly soon during the school year, he would get overlooked for several months. Peter has trouble paying attention to the teacher unless there is some structure around him to remind him when to start an activity and when to make a transition to the next subject. We were very fortunate that Peter had teachers in elementary school who were open to helping him. In the early grades his teachers made sure that he was accepted by the other kids in his class and that there were other students who would help Peter make transitions from one textbook to another and tell him when it was time to leave the classroom for recess, lunch, or the end of the school day.

Middle school was more difficult for Peter. Fellow students became less tolerant of his odd behaviors, and regular class teachers seemed less willing to make accommodations. Although his special education teachers were empathetic and supportive, he spent a large portion of his day in the resource room. By the end of Peter's middle school years, we were looking at his move to high school with considerable trepidation.

During Peter's first term in high school, his special education teacher and several other high school teachers participated in the implementation of the "Putting Feet on My Dreams Project." This curriculum provided information and direction to the teachers and was particularly relevant to Peter's development. In high school Peter has been blessed with very understanding resource room teachers who have done much to facilitate his learning. Peter has done much better academically than we dreamed was possible.

One of Peter's resource teachers is a coach who participated in the project from which this teacher's guide and the accompanying curriculum, "Putting Feet on My Dreams," were developed. He has involved Peter in cross-country, wrestling, and track—athletic activities in which he participates the whole school year. We are amazed and laugh delightedly about "Peter the jock." In his sophomore year his teammates voted Peter as "most inspirational wrestler," and he was awarded a letter for wrestling! Considering the effort Peter must make in relating to others, we continue to be astounded by his success in athletic activities.

We will be forever grateful to the gifted and dedicated teachers Peter has had. They have believed in him and have been a source of continual encouragement. Under their care Peter has blossomed. The available pool of mainstream teachers has been carefully considered, and Peter's resource room teacher has placed him with instructors who have teaching styles compatible with Peter's needs. While he dislikes the hubbub of school, Peter has been responsible about showing up for class. His resource room teacher has helped him to get his assignments done on time. His coaches have worked to instill pride in Peter and acceptance by his teammates. We believe that this teacher's guide and the "Putting Feet on My Dreams" curriculum are providing his teachers and coaches with ideas, direction, and confidence to work effectively with Peter.

It has been a long journey and one that at times has been filled with anxiety as we have pondered Peter's future. Will he be able to hold down a job? What can be expected? All along, Peter has made slow but real progress, and we are cautiously optimistic about his future.

Mary and David Krug, parents

Preface

Our purpose in writing this teacher's guide was twofold: first, to provide special and general education teachers greater insight into their students with autism, and second, to provide strategies for teaching and supporting students with autism more effectively. Many of the examples in this book are centered on the high school years, but the strategies are also effective with elementary, middle school, and postsecondary students.

Because autism is relatively rare, there are few students with autism attending each school and participating in the general education curricula at any one time. As a result, teachers often lack prior experience or specialized knowledge when they need it—namely, when a student with autism is or soon will be attending their classes. We felt that a practical teacher's guide, focused on high school situations, was one way to assist teachers.

As autism specialists we have seen miscommunications and misinterpretations of behavior occur time and again, both on the part of teachers and of students. Often these occur because the student with autism's particular style of thinking, interacting, coping strategies, or intentions are misunderstood. They also occur because students may appear to know what to do in academic or social situations when they do not. These misunderstandings can prevent young persons with autism from attaining their potential and from making the contributions they want to make to their communities.

In order to understand students with autism, teachers need to set aside for a moment what they "know" about adolescents. They need to look with fresh eyes at their student with autism's intentions and resultant actions. In this guide we share insights from young adults with autism and our own teaching experiences to further this process. We then describe strategies for providing assistance in the three areas most needed by students with autism in school. The first of these is the area of instruction and classroom activities. The second is organization and time management. The third is assistance with understanding and participating in social situations. A common feature of these approaches is to provide information visually and in a way that takes into account the student's use of language and style of thinking.

Teachers usually use the term *assistance* to mean something we provide for a while and then gradually discontinue when the student is ready to perform independently. The forms of assistance we describe here are different. They are supports that teachers need to design, maintain, teach their students with autism how to use, and then keep in place. These types of assistance increase independence because students can use the supports to know what to do and when to do it instead of having to rely on continual verbal directions from others. Such strategies can increase the students' success in academic and vocational settings as well as establish strategies to take with them into adulthood.

Our hope in providing this guide is that teachers will gain awareness and practical ideas that they can combine with their own expertise to better teach their students with autism.

Acknowledgments

The development of this guide and a related curriculum—"Putting Feet on My Dreams: A Program in Self-Determination" by A. Fullerton (1994)—was funded by the Office of Special Education and Rehabilitation, U.S. Department of Education Grant PR Award #H158K20019 (1993–1995); under Section 84.158K, Demonstration Projects to Identify & Teach Skills Necessary for Self-Determination. Mike Ward of the U.S Department of Education served as the project officer for the self-determination projects. We thank Mike for his vision and inspiration to us all.

Many thanks to Mary Ann Seaton, Charlotte Duncan, and the Oregon Developmental Disabilities Council for a grant to disseminate an earier version of these materials to parents in Oregon. We also wish to thank the Autism Council of Oregon for its assistance in this effort. Thanks to colleagues at Portland State University—Dave Krug, Steve Edelson, and Ruth Falco—for their support and feedback. Thanks are due also to Jan Allen for her desktop publishing skills.

Working together the authors and illustrator of this guide created a whole that is much greater than any of us could do individually. Ann Fullerton wishes to convey her gratitude and respect to Joyce Stratton, Phyllis Coyne, and Carol Gray, who continually seek to understand the perspectives of their students. Also, to colleague Georgianne Thomas, thank you for your enthusiasm, brilliance, humor, insights, and ability to visually illustrate the concepts and examples we wished to share in this guide. We will long cherish the excitement of working with an artist who could draw our ideas and make them come alive.

Our thanks to Jan Janzen, former Oregon Department of Education statewide autism specialist, for her training, advocacy, and leadership. Our thanks as well to the students with autism who have taught us about themselves and challenged us to learn more. We are also grateful to our colleagues in Oregon's Regional Autism Services for sharing knowledge and providing support.

We wish to thank our partners, friends, and families for their patience and support of our efforts. Thank you, Dean Frost and Tom Thomas.

Most importantly, we thank the young adults who served as participant evaluators in the self-determination project. In sharing your life experiences and perspectives, you have helped many teachers and students understand each other.

Who Are Higher Functioning Young Adults with Autism?

Ann Fullerton

[With thanks to Steve Edelson, Autism Research Institute, San Diego, California, who provided information on the sensory realm.]

This chapter explores the characteristics and experiences of higher functioning persons with autism. We have learned important new information about autism in recent years, thanks in part to the insights shared by persons with autism themselves. A number of these individuals have chosen to describe themselves as "higher functioning persons with autism."

The term *higher functioning* refers to the cognitive ability of the individual. Higher functioning persons with autism have mental abilities in the average to above-average range. Within the higher functioning group, however, there is a wide range in the severity of autistic characteristics. Thus, higher functioning persons with autism may have mild (much like a learning disability), moderate, or severe autism.

A GENERAL DEFINITION OF HIGHER FUNCTIONING AUTISM

The Autism Society of America defines autism as "the result of a neurological disorder that affects functioning of the brain. . . " (Autism Society of America, 1993, p. 3). Donna Williams, a young woman with autism, puts it another way: "Autism is just an information processing problem that controls who I appear to be . . ." (Williams, 1994, p. 238).

Autism is a lifelong developmental disability that typically appears in the first three years of life (Autism Society of America, 1993). Autism is rare, occurring in about 15 of every 10,000 births, and is four times more common in boys than in girls. It is estimated that 25% (Dawson & Castelloe, 1992) to 50% of persons with autism are higher functioning, but at this time such estimates are not based on agreed-upon criteria.

Autism can occur by itself or in combination with other disorders. Autism is not a form of mental retardation or a mental disorder, but it is sometimes misdiagnosed as such, resulting in inappropriate and ineffective treatment. At the present time we do not know what causes autism, but it appears that both genetic factors and neurological damage due to prenatal or birth injury may be involved. Autism is not a result of parenting or emotional trauma (Autism Society of America, 1993).

Some of the behavioral characteristics of higher functioning persons with autism are described below. Some, but not all of these characteristics, might be present in a particular individual. Moreover, these characteristics vary widely in intensity. Each person with autism has a unique blend of strengths and challenges.

BEHAVIORAL CHARACTERISTICS OF AUTISM

- *Differences in the rate of appearance of physical, social, and language skills.* Children with autism may show a scattering of skills and may skip normal developmental steps. A child may develop fine motor skills (e.g., puzzle solving, holding a pencil) before gross motor skills (climbing, running) or vice versa. A child may have a significant delay in learning cause and effect. A student may have exceptional skills in one area of interest. A student may have good word reading, spelling, and math, music, or artistic skills but have difficulty with reading comprehension, story problems, or other cognitive tasks that require creative thinking, cause/effect relationships, judgments, or use of information unrelated to their actual life experience (Janzen, 1986a).

- *Differences in responses to sensory stimuli.* "Any one or a combination of senses or responses are affected: sight, hearing, touch, balance, smell, taste, reaction to pain, and the way a person holds his or her body . . ." (Autism Society of America, 1993, p. 3). Persons with autism may be hyper- or hyposensitive to sensory stimuli and have unusual responses to visual, auditory, or tactile stimuli. They may have difficulty screening out sensory input. They may engage in subtle and not so subtle forms of repetitive behavior (Janzen, 1986a). These may be a release of tension, a response to stress, a way to focus, or a way to control sensory input.

- *Differences in the development of communication.* Persons with autism may have difficulty generating language for fluent, interactive communication. They may have difficulty coordinating the nonverbal behaviors associated with social interaction. Their understanding and use of language may be concrete and literal. They may be confused by words and expressions that depend on the context for meaning (e.g., jokes, sarcasm). They may have difficulty monitoring the reactions of a conversational partner, staying on the topic, and maintaining the conversation (Janzen, 1986a).

- *Differences in ways of relating to people, objects, and events* (Autism Society of America, 1993). Persons with autism may focus on a small detail and have trouble shifting their focus to more critical elements or information.

They may have difficulty sequencing past events yet remember certain events accurately and in great detail. They may have fairly restricted interests. They may be disorganized in time and space. They may develop specific routines for carrying out everyday tasks. They may have difficulty with changes in activities or routines (Janzen, 1993).

As noted earlier, the severity of these characteristics ranges widely in higher functioning persons with autism.

Asperger's syndrome, first described by Asperger in 1994, is a separate developmental disorder that is closely related to higher functioning autism (American Psychiatric Association, 1993). Persons with Asperger's syndrome display one or two of the characteristics described above in milder forms (Dawson & Castelloe, 1992). For example, an individual may develop highly grammatical speech and extensive vocabularies at a young age and at the same time have unusual use of voice and affect as well as difficulty with turn taking or perspective taking in conversation. Persons with Asperger's syndrome may also have learning disabilities in reading, writing, or mathematics. Most of these individuals succeed in academics in school or with the cognitive aspects of their work. However, most have persistent difficulty in understanding social situations, find them challenging and/or uncomfortable (Wing, 1992), and are aware of at least some of their difficulties in the social area.

THREE REALMS OF EXPERIENCE: SENSORY, COGNITIVE, AND SOCIAL

In attempting to describe autism, it is useful to consider the views of family members, teachers, researchers, and especially higher functioning persons with autism themselves. What is often said is that persons with autism process information differently. We will examine this difference in the realms of sensory, cognitive, and social experience. Each of these realms of experience is affected by autism (see Figure 1.1).

For example, in the sensory realm, persons with autism may report sensory perceptions that

FIGURE 1.1. Three Realms of Experience. In this drawing, some of the sensory, cognitive, and social experiences of persons with autism are depicted. In the sensory realm, persons may experience hypersensitive hearing or visual-perceptual challenges. In the cognitive realm, an individual may have a strong visual memory and difficulty organizing abstract information. In the social realm, persons may have difficulty recognizing visual and nonverbal social cues and rules.

differ from those of persons without autism. In the cognitive realm, persons with autism may have excellent memories for factual information but may be challenged by everyday problem solving. In the social realm, the person with autism may have difficulty perceiving what most people would consider to be socially relevant in a situation.

In life, the sensory, cognitive, and social aspects of an experience overlap and influence each other. The same is true here. For example, one's sensory experiences or one's cognitive style can affect one's ability to participate in social situations.

The Sensory Realm

The sensory realm involves how one perceives and learns about the world through one's sensory systems (Figure 1.2). Researchers, parents, and persons with autism have all reported that some persons with autism have differences in their sensory systems. One learns about the world through one's senses. Thus, a different sensory system could result in a different view of the world.

Delacato (1974) was one of the first researchers to speculate that the senses of some persons with autism may be hypersensitive, hyposensitive, or contain white noise. More than one sense may be affected, and both hyper- and hyposensitivities may be experienced at the same time. Some persons with autism report that when there is too much sensory stimulation, they experience sensory overload (Grandin, 1992) and a temporary shutdown of, for example, vision or hearing (Williams, 1994). Another experience that is described is an inability to focus on a specific sensory input if there is too much background sensory input present (e.g., using the phone in an airport) (Grandin & Scariano, 1986). A

FIGURE 1.2. The Sensory Realm. In this realm, persons may experience hypersensitive hearing or visual-perceptual challenges.

related experience of some persons with autism is being unable to shift one's attention from one sensory modality to another (e.g., from visual to auditory input) (Grandin, 1992; Williams, 1994). Studies have shown that some persons with autism have difficulty shifting between different cues in one sensory modality (Wainwright-Sharp & Bryson, 1993), and with shifting attention between sensory modalities (Courchesne, Akshoomoff, & Ciesielski, 1990).

Differences in all the various sensory systems, including the auditory, olfactory, tactile, gustatory, vestibular, and visual systems, have been reported. A brief review of each system is described below. Some but by no means all persons with autism have had these experiences. Some persons report that their sensory sensitivities decreased with age and they suspect that this occurred because they learned to adapt to or cope with the sensitivity. For others, no change occurred with age; and as adults they have made lifestyle choices in order to reduce, for example, the level of auditory stimulation in their home (personal communication, 1992–1993).

Auditory. Common auditory problems are hyperacute hearing, painful hearing, and a constant noise (or tinnitus) interfering with hearing. Hyperacute hearing was the main focus of a book titled *Sound of a Miracle* (Stehli, 1991) in which a mother described her daughter's hypersensitivity to sounds. The daughter, Georgie, could hear some sounds that others could not hear (e.g., water rushing through pipes in the walls) and heard some sounds much louder than others (e.g., rain on the pavement sounded like machine guns). Other parents have reported similar stories, such as their children hearing the neighbors talk in an adjacent house and hearing sirens and airplanes in the distance before others. Collet and his colleagues (1993) recently documented abnormal neurological suppression of auditory stimulation in the brainstem of autistic individuals. They suggested that this lack of suppression may be responsible for sounds being perceived much louder than normal.

Painful hearing also occurs in many people with autism. A survey of over 12,000 parents of autistic children indicated that approximately 40% of their children exhibit some form of painful hearing (Rimland, 1990). Temple Grandin describes her hearing:

> My hearing is like having a hearing aid with the volume control stuck on "super loud." It is like an open microphone that picks up everything. I have two choices; turn the mike on and get deluged with sound, or shut it off. Mother reported that sometimes I acted like I was deaf. Hearing tests indicated that my hearing was normal. I can't modulate incoming auditory stimulation. . . . I still dislike places with confusing noise, such as shopping malls. High-pitched continuous noises such as bathroom vent fans or hair dryers are annoying. I can shut down my hearing and withdraw from most noise, but certain frequencies cannot be shut out. It is impossible for an autistic child to concentrate in a classroom if he is bombarded with noises that blast through his brain like a jet engine . . . . (Grandin, 1992, p. 107)

The notion that some autistic individuals' auditory systems contain noise (tinnitus) was first introduced by Delacato (1974). Although this phenomenon has not been empirically documented, there have been numerous self-reports by autistic children and adults who claim to hear sounds similar to white noise, such as buzzing sounds and motorcycle sounds in their ears (personal communications, 1991–1993). Some individuals have reported a disappearance of these sounds after receiving auditory integration training, a relatively new sound-sensitivity intervention for these individuals (Berard, 1993).

Olfactory. Some persons with autism appear to have hyper- and hyposensitive olfactory systems. Those individuals who are hypersensitive have difficulty with strong perfumes and deodorants, minor house odors, and odorous foods, whereas those individuals who are hyposensitive crave strong odors, such as gasoline. As of this writing, there have not been any studies that have empirically examined this sensory problem.

Tactile. Through the tactile sense, or sense of touch, one can distinguish between a light touch on the skin, different textures, or deep pressure. Some persons with autism have difficulty adjusting to certain tactile sensations. Combinations of hyper- and hyposensitivities are also experienced.

Temple Grandin (1992) reports that it is very hard to adapt to the feel and fit of different clothes. Whereas it might take a person without autism a few minutes, it takes her three to four days. Persons with autism have reported that as children, physical contact from others such as a light touch or hug was physically unpleasant, and so they avoided it (personal communication, 1991–1993). It has been observed that some infants with autism arch their back when they are picked up. It may be that this reaction is based on tactile hypersensitivity and sensory "overload."

Whereas lighter tactile stimulation may be aversive, deeper pressure, when it can be controlled by the individual, may be pleasant and calming. Temple Grandin (1992) describes her experiences. She states that she craved pressure stimulation:

> . . . it was an approach-avoid situation. I wanted to feel the good feeling of being hugged, but when people hugged me the stimuli washed over me like a tidal wave. When I was 5 years old, I used to daydream about a mechanical device I could get into that would apply comforting pressure. Being able to control the device was very important. I had to be able to stop the stimulation when it became too intense. When people hugged me, I stiffened and pulled away to avoid the all-engulfing tidal wave of stimulation. . . . (p. 108)

At age 18, Dr. Grandin designed and built a squeezing machine. A person using the machine could control the amount and duration of pressure applied to the sides of his or her body by pulling a lever (see Grandin and Scariano, 1986, for a description). The deep pressure made possible by the machine can have a very calming effect. Occupational therapists have used Temple's machine with children with autism (Grandin, 1992), as well as other strategies for sensory integration and desensitization (Ayres, 1979).

Gustatory. As is the case with the sense of smell, there is little research but many reports of a unique sense of taste among individuals with autism. Those with hypertaste tend to avoid eating foods with strong flavors and often eat only bland foods. A person may have great difficulty taking medications and vitamins because of their taste.

Vestibular. The vestibular sensory system is connected to the inner ear and provides the body with a sense of balance. A great deal of research has been conducted on the vestibular sense in autism (see Freeman, Frankel, & Ritvo, 1976; Ornitz, 1985). An underaroused vestibular system is considered the primary reason for the rocking behavior of some persons with autism. As adults, many of these individuals actively seek intense vestibular stimulation, such as roller coasters and free-fall rides at amusement parks. In contrast, some people with a hypersensitive vestibular system tend to resist many forms of motion, such as swinging.

Visual. There have been many reports of unusual visual processing in persons with autism. These include difficulty with eye contact, overreliance on peripheral vision, sensitivity to light and color, tunnel vision, and differences in how temporal/spatial relationships are visually perceived.

Some persons with autism are observed to avoid eye contact (Rimland, 1964; Slavik, 1983; Volkmar & Mayes, 1990). Wulf (1994) actually reports that she experiences pain when making prolonged eye contact with other people. By avoiding direct eye contact with others, these individuals rely on observing others using peripheral vision, another characteristic of autism. One autistic man, Gene M., was asked why he looked at people using his peripheral vision, and he replied that "it is like looking through jelly" when looking directly at a person (Marcus, 1992). There is indirect evidence to support the possibility of a dysfunctional visual system in some persons with autism. Creel, Crandell, Pingree, and Ritvo (1989) found abnormal electrical activity in the retina of nearly half of 22 autistic individuals.

Visual hypersensitivity to light and to specific colors has also been observed. Some persons with autism appear to be almost blinded by sunlight and must wear sunglasses in order to see in daylight. There are also reports of children covering their eyes when people wear brightly colored clothing. A number of persons with autism are highly skilled visual artists.

Some persons with autism tend to focus on a specific feature or dimension of an object and have difficulty attending to other nearby features (Lovaas, Koegel, & Schriebman, 1979; Rincover, Feldman, & Eason, 1986). Such "tunnel vision" may limit one's ability to take notice of visual stimuli present in one's environment (Rincover & Ducharme, 1986; Rincover, Feldman, & Eason, 1986). Donna Williams (1992) wrote that she appeared to stare into space as a child, when in actuality she was focusing on the colors emitted from dust particles. In visual perception experiments, some higher functioning persons with autism may miss or respond more slowly to rapidly changing and novel visual cues than persons without autism (Wainwright-Sharp & Bryson, 1993).

Melvin Kaplan has studied the visual systems of autistic individuals for many years and has suggested that persons with autism as well as other individuals with neurological problems have difficulty processing temporal/spatial relationships. Such visual perception problems can lead to difficulties moving in and interacting with the physical environment. Kaplan suggests that the characteristics of some children with autism, such as toe walking, or unusual posture or balance, can be explained by differences in the visual system (Kaplan, in preparation).

Recently, Donna Williams (1993) has described the visual perception she experiences. She reports that scenes and objects are fragmented and she cannot distinguish between the foreground and background. Donna was not aware that she saw things differently until she tried corrective lenses. According to her, the lenses allowed her to look directly at an object, scene, or person and see the parts and whole as one, integrated perception. Looking at her friend Paul, she reports:

> . . . Paul's face was joined together. His eyes and nose and mouth and chin were all held together with equal impact in a single context. Then I noticed that his neck and shoulders and torso and legs were also joined, not bit by bit as my eyes moved along, but as a whole picture, like captured by a camera. Paul was joined together and he looked great. (Williams, 1994, pp. 7–8)

Summary of the Sensory Realm. At the present time it is not clear what neurological differences underlie these sensory experiences. The source of this difference does not seem to lie in the sensory organs (eyes, ears); these appear to be intact in persons with autism (Hermelin & O'Connor, 1970). Instead, recent studies have suggested that portions of the brain that may regulate sensory input may be different in persons with autism (Bauman & Kemper, 1994).

In Figure 1.3, some of the sensory experiences that different persons with autism have reported are illustrated. In the innermost ring is a person. The next ring depicts various sensory sensitivities. The next ring illustrates what the person might think or wish he or she could do in response to these sensory experiences. The outermost ring portrays what the person chooses to do instead in order to cope with these experiences in a social world.

FIGURE 1.3. Some of the sensory experiences of some persons with autism.

The Cognitive Realm

The cognitive realm includes attending, learning, remembering, and problem solving. The preceding description of the sensory realm indicated that many persons with autism perceive and process sensory information differently. What this means is that the information or "raw material" one has available to think about is different. If one takes in different information than others, then it follows that one will reach different conclusions. In highly complex ways our sensory processes and our cognitive processes are intertwined. Researchers are just beginning to explore the implications of the sensory system of people with autism on their cognitive development.

Cognitive Style. Apart from these sensory-cognitive relationships, researchers have also noted that individuals with autism have a different cognitive style. In this section we turn to accounts and descriptions of this particular style (see Figure 1.4). This cognitive

FIGURE 1.4. The Cognitive Realm. In the cognitive realm, an individual may have a strong visual memory and difficulty organizing abstract information.

style is described as one in which information is taken in with little analysis or integration (Prizant 1983; Frith, 1989; Janzen, 1993). All of the aspects of an experience are taken in and may be remembered with equal significance. The person with autism has difficulty extracting from the situation what others would see as most relevant, functional, or meaningful.

Jan Janzen (in preparation) has used the analogy of a video camera to describe what it would be like to take everything in.[1] Think for a moment of the brain as a super recording device that takes in every sight, sound, touch, taste, and odor, in minute detail. The person with autism has difficulty controlling the device to

analyze or "edit" the tape to screen out irrelevant material, it is all stored randomly and unintegrated into single separate units. . . . If the camera is on, everything goes in. If it is off, nothing goes in. Sometimes the camera is turned on and off quickly, so the event is stored as a short unit (a snapshot). Other units are longer. . . . with no relationship to the actual beginning or end of the event. Sometimes the lens is focused on something of particular interest to the individual while relevant information is described or modeled by the teacher in a different

---

[1]This analogy is expanded in the book: Janzen, J. E. (in preparation). *Understanding the nature of autism: Strategies for parents and teachers*, Tucson, AZ: Communication Therapy Skill Builders.

part of the room. . . . Whatever is recorded, is stored. It is easy to see why the world is so confusing for them. . . . (Janzen, 1993, p. 8)

In this analogy, Janzen has described how the person with autism may attend to and remember information.

Once information is received, how then is it used to solve problems? In order to explore this question, Uta Frith (1989) has compared the way children with and without autism solve cognitive tasks. She suggests that persons without autism ". . . have a built-in propensity to form coherence over as wide a range of stimuli as possible or as wide a range of contexts as possible . . ." (Frith, 1989, p. 100). Persons with autism, however, may not perceive or use the overall context, meaning, or structure available to solve a cognitive task.

Sometimes, not seeing the overall context can be useful. For example, if asked to find a triangle shape hidden in a picture of a baby buggy, children with autism may find the hidden shape more easily than children without autism (Frith, 1989). Some children with autism can memorize a meaningful sentence and a radom list of words equally well.

Children *without* autism, however, find it harder to remember random list of words than meaningful sentences (Frith, 1989). These findings suggest that the child with autism may not perceive or use the overall meaning to be found in a problem in order to solve the problem (Frith, 1989). The cognitive style described by Janzen (in preparation) and Frith (1989) is reflected in how persons with autism attend, learn, remember, and solve problems.

Attending. Persons with autism are able to attend and to sustain their attention, but they may have difficulty controlling their attention. It may be hard to activate their attention, to stay focused, or to flexibly shift their attention when it is adaptive to do so (Rumsey, 1992). For example, some higher functioning persons with autism may find it difficult to rapidly scan stimulus materials and make a quick response (Rumsey, 1992). Higher functioning persons with autism can

also have difficulty when a task requires them to shift their attention in midstream (Rumsey, 1992).

On the other hand, some higher functioning persons with autism do very well on tasks that require one to stay focused on and manipulate numerical information (Rumsey & Hamburger, 1988). Some may also perform well on other tasks that require sustained attention. Thus, persons with autism have strengths and also face challenges in the act of attending.

Memory and Learning. Many persons with autism have excellent long-term memories and can recall in minute detail events that occurred years before. This has been considered to be a form of eidetic memory, in which all aspects of an event are stored and can later be fully retrieved. Often higher functioning persons with autism have excellent rote memories and learn new factual, concrete information accurately after a single presentation. However, they may not attach meaning to the information (Janzen, 1986b).

When remembering larger amounts of information, such as a paragraph, persons with autism may have difficulty immediately recalling the paragraph but do benefit from rehearsal such that the more they repeat information the better they can remember it at a later time (Rumsey, 1992). This suggests that they are encoding the words at a literal level, whereas persons without autism use associative or semantic features in order to remember in both the short and the long run (Rumsey, 1992). Thus, "rote memory, unaltered by active encoding or deeper levels of processing may be characteristic of autism . . ." (Rumsey, 1992, p. 47).

How is this different from the way the person without autism remembers? Cognitive theorists speculate that when one remembers something, one encodes it in some way. Encoding means that the new information is organized in ways that are meaningful to the person and tied to prior knowledge, thereby making it easier to retrieve later when needed.

Researchers believe that when persons without autism store information, it is associated with a social context and in a temporal relationship to other events. Because one makes meaning of something in order to remember it, one selectively remembers only parts of the event. Persons with autism may "encode" differently. One man with autism speculated, ". . . I think most normal people have a memory that is like a continuum. Mine is just like up here. I can remember something but I don't remember what came before or after . . ." (McDonnell, 1991). Donna Williams describes her memory in discussing a conversation with her therapist/teacher:

> He thought he could help me find different ways to tackle various problem situations. I couldn't really see how he could help though. I would learn how to tackle a given situation in one context but be lost when confronted by the same situation in another context. Things just didn't translate. If I learned something while I was standing with a woman in the kitchen and it was summer and it was daytime, the lesson wouldn't be triggered in a similar situation if I was standing with a man in another room and it was winter and it was nighttime. Things were stored but the compulsive over-categorization of them was so refined that events had to be close to identical to be considered comparable. . . . (Williams, 1994, pp. 64–65)

Problem Solving. Some higher functioning persons with autism have difficulty with a wide range of problem solving tasks. They may understand the language involved in the problem and have excellent visioperceptual skills but run into difficulty because they don't integrate information to draw inferences (Rumsey & Hamburger, 1988). On other problem solving tasks, they may repeat the same errors and have difficulty learning from experience (Hoffmann & Prior, 1982). These challenges with problem solving tasks are less evident in persons with Asperger's syndrome (Rumsey, 1992).

In everyday life we often need to problem solve. In the following passage a woman with autism describes her experience in a job indexing newspaper articles. She describes two challenges that she faced: (1) knowing that she needed to organize information but not having the social knowledge with which to make judgments and (2) having difficulty coordinating the multiple aspects of the task.

> I started indexing the Chicago Times at home on a part-time basis. However, I was unable to deal with the subtle nuances of the work: Which subject heading should I use? Should I index this editorial? I could not figure out the answers. This was a problem I had had in other jobs as well. I could not generalize from one situation to another and could not deal with the many complexities involved in any one task—a typical problem in autistic people. I was let go from this job primarily for that reason, although my supervisor greatly admired my work and wanted me to continue. . . . (Carpenter, 1992, p. 292)

Visual Thinking. Some persons with autism describe themselves and are observed to be strong visual thinkers. They have excellent ability to remember and retrieve visual images. Some young adults with autism have become aware that they cannot remember long strings of auditory information. When too much and too long a string of verbal information comes their way, they "shut down," but when the same information is presented visually in pictures and words, they know what to do. These individuals ask others to write down the steps in a task for them so that they can learn the task (Williams, 1992; Grandin, 1992).

Temple Grandin states, ". . . [A]ll my thinking is visual. When I think about abstract concepts such as getting along with people, I use visual images such as the sliding glass door. Relationships must be approached carefully otherwise the sliding door could be shattered" (Grandin, 1992, p. 116). Grandin is a professor in animal husbandry and has built an international consulting business designing livestock processing plants. She notes that "visual thinking is an asset for an equipment designer. I am able to 'see' how all the parts of a project will fit together and see potential problems . . ." (p. 116). ". . . I am able to visualize a motion picture of the finished facility in my imagination . . ." (p. 117).

Another young woman with autism has made an insightful link between "taking things literally" and her use of visualization to think about and organize information:

> Visualization is very helpful for me. Because I visualize, I often take things literally. Someone once asked me, "Where are you?" and I said, "Massachusetts." She said, "What do you want most out of life?" and I said, "a hamburger." It would have been much better for me if she had said, "Where are you in regard to your personal development in life and the universe?" When you get a literal answer, it may be due to the sentence being misinterpreted or the sentence not being long enough. It makes a difference in how a question is answered if a single adverb or adjective is left out. . . . (Lissner, 1992, p. 306)

These persons with autism are suggesting that they think in pictures and visual images rather than in words that are laden with socially based symbolic meanings. Thus, if Ms. Lissner is translating the words spoken to her into her visual images for those words, then she is likely to interpret the meaning and intention of the speaker's question differently.

Janzen suggests that persons with autism have difficulty "organizing information for themselves but if it is organized visually to highlight the meaning, relationships, and sequences, they learn remarkably fast" (Janzen, 1993).

Summary of the Cognitive Realm. Higher functioning persons with autism have a particular cognitive style that is reflected in their cognitive abilities and challenges. We will examine these in more detail in Chapters 3 and 4 when we explore ways to provide instructional and organizational assistance.

The Social Realm

The social realm includes language, communication, and social interaction. At the present time, the communicative and social aspects of autism are its most salient characteristics. For persons with autism, communication and social interaction are often the most challenging aspects of living with autism (Grandin, 1992; Sinclair, 1992; Williams, 1992, 1994).

Social interaction is extremely complex and multifaceted. It involves language, physical, and cognitive components. One must understand the meaning of spoken language within the context in which it occurs. One must be able to perceive the nonverbal social cues of others and be able to control and respond with one's own multiple nonverbal behaviors. And lastly, one must be able to interpret these verbal and nonverbal behaviors in an ongoing social context (see Figure 1.5).

At all of these levels, research and personal accounts suggest that persons with autism face challenges. Coordinating these complex components of social interaction comes naturally to most persons without autism. In contrast, some persons with autism see themselves as lacking these "basic instincts which make communication a natural process" (Cesaroni & Garber, 1991, p. 311). As Temple Grandin states, ". . . I had to learn social interaction skills by using my intellect . . ." (Grandin, 1992, p. 7).

Language Use in Communication. Higher functioning persons with autism often learn to read at an early age and develop excellent vocabularies. At times, however, they may use this language at a higher level than they fully understand. They may have difficulty understanding the meaning of words or concepts they have not directly experienced (Janzen, 1986b).

For example, persons with autism can be confused when the meaning of a word depends on the context in which it is used. Thus, the use of pronouns (he, she), time and space concepts (later, after), and homonyms, or words that sound the same (blue-blew, their-there), can be misunderstood. This has been characterized as using language literally (as described by Kathy Lissner above). Expressions such as "save your breath," "jump the gun," and "second thoughts" may be confusing (Moreno, 1991).

FIGURE 1.5. The Social Realm. In the social realm, persons with autism may have difficulty recognizing verbal and nonverbal social cues and rules.

Persons with autism have reported difficulty understanding words such as *feel* and *know* (Sinclair, 1992). Donna Williams says that "the words 'know' and 'feel' were like 'it' and 'of' and 'by'—you couldn't see them or touch them, so the meaning wasn't significant. People cannot show you a 'know' and you cannot see what 'feel' looks like . . . " (Williams, 1994, p. 68).

A higher functioning person with autism may also be confused by humor and sarcasm—aspects of language laden with hidden social meanings. Dewey (1980) described a young man who became aware that he did not understand the jokes in humorous cartoons. Wishing to correct this, he studied cartoons and discussed their meaning with his parents for

several years until he could explain "the point of almost any cartoon" (Dewey, 1980, p. 1). He made this great effort so that he could do what came so easily to others (Dewey, 1980).

Persons with autism sometimes develop very specific interests, study them extensively, and then choose a narrow focus and very few topics in their conversations. In everyday discourse, higher functioning persons with autism may not be aware of or have difficulty monitoring other people's level of interest in what they are saying (Williams, 1994). The reasons for these intense interests may not be clear to the persons themselves (Lissner, 1992). This ability to pursue one's interests, however, is a potential strength and can be directed into significant life pursuits and employment (Grandin, 1992). For example, Temple Grandin (1992) said that a high school teacher helped her develop her interest in cattle chutes into her international consulting business designing livestock processing plants.

Donna Williams describes herself as "meaning-deaf"; she hears the sounds but not the meaning of the sounds (Williams, 1994, p. 50). Donna states that she had a huge vocabulary and could memorize and mimic entire conversations. But only after years of effort did she begin to "hear with meaning" at least the key words spoken during a conversation. She says:

> As a result I am learning to feel like a part of things . . . and can really understand why people communicate; but although my ability to speak is great, my ability to converse is still not good. . . . I think these communication things are the things that were missing, that I've been trying to find. . . . (Williams, 1994, p. 100)

In order to have a reciprocal conversation, the speakers construct shared meaning by referring to information that is common to both. Communication fails when this process breaks down (Fine, Bartolucci, Szatmari, & Ginsberg, 1994). Linguistic analysis of the speech of nonautistic persons, higher functioning persons with autism, and persons with Asperger's syndrome reveals that all three groups share information equally often when conversing. However, the higher functioning person with autism refers more often to the physical world and less often to previous comments in the conversation. The communication strategies used by persons with Asperger's syndrome are essentially the same as those of persons without autism. Individuals with Asperger's syndrome, however, may more frequently refer to other things that are unclear within the context of the immediate conversation (Fine et al., 1994).

These examples illustrate some of the challenges persons with autism and with Asperger's syndrome encounter with the semantic (meaning) and the pragmatic (social) features of language.

The Ability To Control the Subtle Behaviors of Social Interaction. Another aspect of social interaction is the complex nonverbal interchanges that occur between people. These nonverbal social behaviors require physical movements. We use complex, subtle, and highly coordinated facial expressions, gestures, and vocal intonations when we interact.

As early as infancy, differences in such nonverbal social behaviors are observed in persons with autism. At one year of age, infants with autism may not look at others, show objects to others, gaze back and forth between a desired object and a person (known as joint attention), or orient toward the sound of their name being called as often as infants without autism (Osterling & Dawson, 1994). Toddlers with autism gaze at their mothers and smile at their mothers as often and for the same length of time as children without autism (Dawson & Galpert, 1990). However, they are less likely to coordinate their smiles with eye contact in a single act that conveys communicative intent. In addition, they smile *in response to* their mothers' smile less often (Dawson & Galpert, 1990).

Different infants with autism have highly individual, unique, vocalizations (Ricks, 1975). The facial expressions of children with autism are more often composed of unusual blends of emotions (Kasari, Sigman, Mundy, & Yirmiya, 1990). Children with autism display as many attention-getting and goal-requesting gestures, but fewer of the gestures one associates with expressing social affect than developmentally delayed children (Attwood, Frith, & Hermelin, 1988).

These differences continue into adulthood for some persons with autism. Studies of older persons with autism suggest that some individuals "may not be able to control their own vocal intonation and facial expression to convey the emotions they feel, leading others to misperceive him or her as unfeeling or aloof . . . " (Rumsey, 1992, p. 42).

The social interchanges between people are like a dance; they occur at a certain pace, and the timing of each person's actions is important. Studies indicate that persons with autism have difficulty with this interpersonal coordination (Attwood, Frith, & Hermelin, 1988; Kasari, Sigman, Mundy, & Yirmiya, 1990). Newson (1980) suggests that some persons with autism have difficulty with "the way people's actions fit in or 'mesh' with each other, both within one person and between people." She notes that this "timing is absolutely essential to our *use* of messages, to create a conversational flow . . ."(p. 1).

Williams (1994) says that the pace of social interactions can make it difficult for persons with autism to catch everything that happens. As noted in the review of the sensory realm, persons with autism may need more time to shift between auditory and visual cues. Grandin (1992) suspects that as a result, persons with autism can have difficulty following the interchanges in a social interaction.

Lawrie Horner provides a picture of what she experiences in social situations and what strategies she uses to make them more optimal for her:

> . . . I find the most difficult social situations are those where I have different relationships with different people, where some people know each other and others don't, where there is no formal activity and so I have to respond as best I can to the utterly confusing social cues, where there is some sense of occasion and everyone is in a sense acting up to that occasion. A perfect example is a cocktail party. I can say for a fact that I get more, socially, from a visit to the dentist than from organized social events. . . .

> . . . I've learnt a couple of things about social events. One is not to try and do more than I really can. This means that I hang around in the background and chat briefly with one or two people as they go past, and I don't bother trying to be part of a group. I try to ignore the bizarre impressions that people give me socially—the facial and vocal contortions, the sudden moves of eye, gesture, and head which they do so easily and which

strike me as so sudden and confusing. I try not to get fixated on people's hands, waving so distractingly and strangely. I find the hardest thing is to avoid getting paranoid. I always get the impression that everyone is watching me fumbling away in the background and that everyone is talking about me. They may be, of course. (Horner, 1993, p. 22)

Social Perception. Social perception includes the ability to perceive emotional expressions and other social cues. We recognize and react to human socio-emotional cues very early in life. For example, by seven months of age, babies notice when facial expressions and vocal expressions match or don't match (Hobson, 1992).

Studies have found that some persons with autism have difficulty reading vocal or facial expressions. Some higher functioning adults with autism are less able to name the emotions in speech samples, identify the affect in photos of faces, as well as match these with contexts that might elicit each emotion (Macdonald et al. 1989). They also have greater difficulty than persons without autism in matching descriptive words with pictures that show a part of a face expressing the same emotional content (Hobson & Lee, 1989). In some cases they are less able to perceive age and sex-related characteristics of persons in pictures (Hobson, 1987).

These research findings highlight some differences in persons with autism but do not explain these differences. Indeed, persons with autism may go about discriminating different facial expressions in their own way, using their own abilities. For example, young adults with autism are better than young adults without autism at identifying emotions in pictures of whole faces that are upside down! (Hobson & Lee, 1989). Further research of visual perception may clarify why some higher functioning persons have difficulty discriminating facial, gestural, and vocal emotional expressions and recognizing how different expressions are coordinated with each other (Hobson, 1992).

Wing (1992) reports that one young man with autism said with great sadness: "People give each other messages with their eyes but I don't know what they are saying . . ." (p. 131).

Social Cognition. Perhaps the most mysterious aspect of our ability to interact with others is how we know what to do in social situations, infer the intentions of others, empathize with others, interpret social cues, and see another person's point of view. These are all aspects of social cognition.

Persons with autism and their parents and teachers have noted that understanding and learning from social events is a particular challenge. Social situations are full of subtle cues, unspoken rules, and meanings derived from the social context. Although social situations are very complex, most persons without autism seem to have an ability to interpret and "know what to do" in social situations with ease.

One young woman with autism explains:

It is very difficult for even a higher functioning autistic adult to know exactly when to say something, when to ask for help, or when to remain quiet. To such a person, life is a game in which the rules are constantly changing without rhyme or reason. (Carpenter, 1992, p. 291)

Studies have found that some children with autism seem to have difficulty identifying what other people know in a situation. This has been studied in various experimental situations (Baron-Cohen, 1989; Frith, 1989). For example, children with autism watch as an object is taken from a box and hidden in a closet. Later, a person who has not seen this occur enters the room. When the children with autism are asked "Where will this person look for the object?" some children say "the closet." Thus the children answer as if they think the other person knows the same things that they do. This result has been interpreted to mean that some, but not all, children with autism have difficulty knowing the mental states of others (Baron-Cohen, 1989).

An alternative possibility is that persons with autism focus on a portion rather than the overall situation or context (Happe, 1994). In another study, adults were presented with stories about everyday situations where people say things they do not mean literally. Compared to persons without autism, some of the adults

with autism had difficulty predicting what people in the story would say or explaining why they would say those things (Happe, 1994). Upon close analysis, it appears that these adults gave answers that fit with a portion of the story but did not fit the overall social context in the story. This is consistent with Frith's (1989) theory that some persons with autism have difficulty using the most coherent, overall information available in a situation.

Developmental theorists argue that social cognition (such as the perspective taking just described) begins with the infant's and toddler's desire and ability to imitate others, engage others in interaction, and use symbolic play. "The child with autism engages in less spontaneous imitation of others. This may interfere with the development of reciprocity, joint attention, and awareness of emotional and mental states in self and others" (Klinger & Dawson, 1992, p. 383). By nine months of age, infants point things out to their mothers and look back and forth between the object and their mothers' eyes (Klinger & Dawson, 1992). It seems that the infants are trying to get mom to think about the same thing they are thinking about. This is called having "joint attention." In some cases, young children with autism are less likely to try to get others to engage in joint attention with them (Klinger & Dawson, 1992). Some children with autism engage in little symbolic play, and others develop symbolic play later than children without autism (Jarrold, Boucher, & Smith, 1993).

Dawson and her colleagues have proposed a possible reason children with autism do not engage in these early social behaviors (Klinger & Dawson, 1992). Humans are born with complex and sensitive sensory systems through which they take in all types of environmental stimulation. To control this potential bombardment, humans also have innate neurological systems that regulate their level of arousal and help them orient toward and detect novel stimuli. Research suggests that these neurological systems may not work as well in children with autism. Thus, they may be too easily overaroused and have a very narrow range of optimal stimulation within which they are able to attend to stimuli. Perhaps when stimulation is too great, the child with autism withdraws and stops attending (Klinger & Dawson, 1992).

Many children with autism actively explore and learn about physical objects upon which they can repeat the same actions. It may be that because mechanical events with objects are predictable and in the child's control, these events can be more easily assimilated and are less likely to elicit overarousal and inattention (Klinger & Dawson, 1992). In contrast, "social, emotional, and linguistic stimuli are, by nature, relatively unpredictable and indeterminate" (Klinger & Dawson, 1992, p. 165). This may be the reason that the child with autism has difficulty processing social information, such as vocalizations, gestures, and facial expressions. "Without the ability to impose meaning upon the ever-changing flow of social information, the person with autism may be overwhelmed and over-aroused by such information, and respond by failing to attend or even withdrawing from such stimuli" (Klinger & Dawson, 1992, pp. 165–166).

Summary of the Social Realm. Persons with autism face challenges in many aspects of social functioning. Some individuals have difficulty with the semantics of language and with conversational flow. The multiple nonverbal behaviors involved in social interaction can be hard to perceive and to coordinate. Persons with autism may also have difficulty inferring what other people are thinking or feeling. At the present time it is not clear why these challenges occur. They may begin in infancy and be related to sensory perception and cognitive style. Chapter 4 provides methods for helping young adults with autism to gain social knowledge.

UNDERSTANDING THE PERSPECTIVE OF PERSONS WITH AUTISM

The social realm just described is a two-way street. One of the most important messages in this guide is that *when one strives to teach and befriend a person with autism one must set aside the notion that one knows why people do what they do.*

As social beings, humans observe and interpret the actions of others based on their own previous stockpile of social and personal experiences. People tend to feel certain emotions automatically when others do or say certain things. This is an important part of being a socially adept and sensitive person.

Thus people constantly make judgments in social relationships. Most people think that they know other persons' intentions when they do or say something. For example, if a person acts aloof and won't look at us, then we assume he or she doesn't want to talk to us or doesn't like us. If a person talks constantly and never lets us get a word in edgewise, then we assume the other person wants to dominate the conversation or be the center of attention. In typical social experience, this is often what these actions mean. But with persons with autism, this is often the wrong interpretation.

Donna Williams describes what she learned from her psychologist/teacher about the differences between herself and others:

> He tried to explain gently to me that other people generally didn't have these difficulties, and that was why they hadn't understood. He explained how other people got all the bits working at once. How they managed to get the mechanics of so many things going at the same time was nothing short of a miracle. . . . No wonder, in the face of my apparent intelligence, they were surprised and angered that they weren't making any sense to me and so assumed I wasn't listening or didn't want to. No wonder they were confused and hurt as to why I could talk so well and yet not converse "with" and so assumed I was merely selfish or arrogant as I continued rigidly on my own topics. No wonder they didn't know how I felt if I couldn't get emotional expression and words going at the same time and figured I didn't care or had no feelings. . . . (Williams, 1994, p. 86)

CHAPTER SUMMARY

Higher functioning persons with autism process information differently. This difference is neurologically based and evident at a very young age. A wide array of research findings, parent and teacher observations, and personal experiences of persons with autism have been described in this chapter. These were organized into three realms—sensory, cognitive, and social experiences—although it is clear that these overlap in complex ways.

It is important to remember that each individual with autism is unique and may or may not experience all of the sensory, cognitive, and social challenges described here. Higher functioning persons with autism have average to above-average mental abilities but vary widely in the severity and number of challenges they face due to autism. In terms of everyday functioning, some persons need little or no assistance, whereas others need daily assistance in various forms.

Recent discoveries have greatly increased our understanding of autism. The insights provided by higher functioning persons with autism are especially significant. With this new information, persons with and without autism are now better able to understand each other.

REFERENCES

American Psychiatric Association. (1993). *Diagnostic and statistical manual of mental disorders* (4th ed.). Washington, DC: Author.

Attwood, A., Frith, U., & Hermelin, B. (1988). The understanding and use of interpersonal gestures by autistic and Down's syndrome children. *Journal of Autism and Developmental Disorders, 18*, 241–257.

Autism Society of America, Inc. (1993). Definition of autism. *The Advocate: Newsletter of the Autism Society of America, Inc.* Silver Spring, MD.

Ayres, J. A. (1979). *Sensory integration and the child.* Los Angeles: Western Psychological Services.

Baron-Cohen, S. (1989). The autistic child's theory of mind: A case of specific developmental delay. *Journal of Child Psychology and Psychiatry, 30*, 285–298.

Bauman, M. L., & Kemper, T. L. (1994). Neuroanatomic observations of the brain in autism. In M. L. Bauman & T. L. Kemper (Eds), *The neurobiology in autism.* Baltimore: Johns Hopkins University Press.

Berard, G. (1993). *Hearing equals behavior.* New Canaan, CT: Keats.

Carpenter, A. (1992). Personal essays. In E. Schopler & G. B. Mesibov (Eds.), *High-functioning individuals with autism* (pp. 289–294). New York: Plenum.

Cesaroni, L., & Garber, M. (1991). Exploring the experience of autism through firsthand accounts. *Journal of Autism and Developmental Disorders, 21*(3), 303–313.

Collett, L., Roge, B., Descouens, D., Moron, P., Duverdy, F., & Urgell, H. (1993). Objective auditory dysfunction in infantile autism. *The Lancet, 342*, 923.

Courchesne, E., Akshoomoff, N. A., & Ciesielski, K. T. (1990). *Shifting attention abnormalities in autism: ERP and performance evidence.* Poster presented at the meeting of the International Neuropsychological Society, Orlando, FL.

Creel, D. J., Crandall, A. S., Pingree, C., & Ritvo, E. R. (1989). Abnormal electroretinograms in autism. *Clinical Vision Science, 4*, 85–88.

Dawson, G., & Castelloe, P. (1992). Autism. In C. E. Walker & M. C. Roberts, (Eds.), *Handbook of clinical child psychology* (pp. 375–397). New York: John Wiley & Sons.

Dawson, G., & Galpert, L. (1990). Mothers' use of imitative play for facilitating social responsiveness and toy play in young autistic children. *Development and Psychopathology, 2*, 151–162.

Delacato, C. H. (1974). *The ultimate stranger.* Novato, CA: Academic Therapy.

Dewey, M. A. (1980). *The socially aware autistic adult and child.* Talk given at Warwick Conference (September).

Fine, J., Bartolucci, G., Szatmari, P., & Ginsberg, G. (1994). Cohesive discourse in pervasive developmental disorders. *Journal of Autism and Developmental Disorders, 24*(3), 315–329.

Freeman, B. J., Frankel, F., & Ritvo, E. R. (1976). The effects of response contingent vestibular stimulation on the behavior of autistic and retarded children. *Journal of Autism and Childhood Schizophrenia, 6*, 353–358.

Frith, U. (1989). *Autism: Explaining the enigma.* Oxford: Blackwell.

Grandin, T. (1992). An inside view of autism. In E. Schopler & G. B. Mesibov (Eds.), *High-functioning individuals with autism* (pp. 105–126). New York: Plenum.

Grandin, T., & Scariano, M. M. (1986). *Emergence labeled autistic*. Novato, CA: Arena.

Happe, F. G. E. (1994). An advanced test of theory of mind: Understanding of story characters' thoughts and feelings by able autistic, mentally handicapped, and normal children and adults. *Journal of Autism and Developmental Disorders, 24*(2), 129–154.

Hermelin, B., & O'Connor, N. (1970). *Psychological experiments with autistic children*. Oxford: Pergamon.

Hobson, R.P. (1987). The autistic child's recognition of age- and sex-related characteristics of people. *Journal of Autism and Developmental Disorders, 17*, 63–79.

Hobson, R. P. (1992). Social perception in high-level autism. In E. Schopler & G. B. Mesibov (Eds.), *High-functioning individuals with autism* (pp. 157–184). New York: Plenum.

Hobson, R. P., & Lee, A. (1989). Emotion-related and abstract concepts in autistic people: Evidence from the British Picture Vocabulary Scale. *Journal of Autism and Developmental Disorders, 19*, 601–623.

Hoffmann, W. L., & Prior, M. R. (1982). Neuropsychological dimensions of autism in children: A test of the hemispheric dysfunction hypothesis. *Journal of Clinical Neuropsychology, 4*, 27–41.

Horner, L. (1993). Some things which work and some which don't and why I'm happy being autistic. *Our Voice: The Newsletter of the Autism International Network, 2*, 19–23.

Janzen, J. (1986a). *The high functioning student with autism. Part. I: Overview* (Unpublished manuscript FYI 06). Available from Oregon Department of Education State Regional Program for Students with Autism, 700 Pringle Parkway SE, Salem, OR 97310.

Janzen, J. (1986b). *The high functioning student with autism. Part II: Teaching and problem solving* (Unpublished manuscript FYI 07). Available from Oregon Department of Education State Regional Program for Students with Autism, 700 Pringle Parkway SE, Salem, Oregon 97310.

Janzen, J. E. (1993). Understanding autism in the young child: Practical intervention strategies.

Rapsource Access Project 8(2). School of Extended Studies, Portland State University, P.O. Box 1491, Portland, OR.

Jarrold, C., Boucher, J., & Smith, P. (1993). Symbolic play in autism: A review. *Journal of Autism and Developmental Disorders, 23*(2), 281–307.

Kaplan, M. (In preparation). *Visual model for children with neurointegrative dysfunction*. Manuscript in preparation for publication.

Kasari, C., Sigman, M., Mundy, P., & Yirmiya, N. (1990). Affective sharing in the context of joint attention interactions of normal, autistic, and mentally retarded children. *Journal of Autism and Developmental Disorders, 20*, 87–100.

Klinger, L. G., & Dawson, G. (1992). Facilitating early social and communicative development in children with autism. In S. F. Warren & J. Reichle (Eds.), *Causes and effects in communication and language intervention* (pp. 157–186). Baltimore: Paul H. Brookes.

Lissner, K. (1992). Insider's point of view. In E. Schopler & G. B. Mesibov (Eds.), *High-functioning individuals with autism* (pp. 303–306). New York: Plenum.

Lovaas, O.I., Koegel, R.L., & Schriebman, L. (1979). Stimulus overselectivity in autism: A review of research. *Psychological Bulletin, 86*, 1236–1254.

Macdonald, H., Rutter, M., Howlin, P., Rios, P., LeCouteur, A., Evered, C., & Folstein, S. (1989). Recognition and expression of emotional cues by autistic and normal adults. *Journal of Child Psychology and Psychiatry, 30*, 865–877.

McDonnell, P. (1991). *About our lives: Young adults with autism speak out*. Panel at the National Conference of the Autism Society of America, July 9, 1991.

Moreno, S. J. (1991). *High-functioning individuals with autism: Advice and information for parents and others who care*. Crown Point, IN: Maap Services.

Newson, E. (1980). *The socially aware autistic child and adult*. Talk given at Warwick Conference (September).

Ornitz, E. M. (1985). Neurophysiology of infantile autism. *Journal of American Academy of Child Psychiatry, 24*, 251–262.

Osterling, J., & Dawson, G. (1994). Early recognition of children with autism: A study of first birthday home videotapes. *Journal of Autism and Developmental Disorders, 24*(3), 247–257.

Prizant, B. M. (1983). Language acquisition and communicative behavior in autism: Toward an understanding of the "whole" of it. *Journal of Speech and Hearing Disorders, 48,* 296–307.

Ricks, D. M. (1975). Vocal communication in pre-verbal normal and autistic children. In N. O'Connor (Ed.), *Language, cognitive deficits and retardation* (pp. 75–80). London: Butterworths.

Rimland, B. (1990). Sound sensitivity in autism. *Autism Research Review International, 4,* 3, 6.

Rimland, B. (1964). *Infantile autism.* New York: Appleton-Century-Crofts.

Rincover, A., & Ducharme, J. M. (1986). Variables influencing stimulus overselectivity and "tunnel vision" in developmentally delayed children. *American Journal of Mental Deficiency, 91,* 422–430.

Rincover, A., Feldman, M., & Eason, L. (1986). Tunnel vision: A possible keystone stimulus control deficit in autistic children. *Analysis and intervention in developmental disabilities, 6,* 283–307.

Rumsey, J. M. (1992). Neuropsychological studies of high-level autism. In E. Schopler & G. B. Mesibov (Eds.), *High-functioning individuals with autism* (pp. 41–64). New York: Plenum.

Rumsey, J. M., & Hamburger, S. D. (1988). Neuropsychological findings in high-functioning men with infantile autism, residual state. *Journal of Clinical and Experimental Neuropsychology, 10,* 201–221.

Sinclair, J. (1992). Bridging the gaps: An inside-out view of autism (or, Do you know what I don't know?). In E. Schopler & G. B. Mesibov (Eds.), *High-functioning individuals with autism* (pp. 294–302). New York: Plenum.

Slavik, B. A. (1983). Vestibular stimulation and eye contact in autistic children. *American Journal of Occupational Therapy, 37,* 17.

Stehli, A. (1991). *The sound of a miracle.* New York: Doubleday.

Volkmar, F. R., & Mayes, L. C. (1990). Gaze behavior in autism. *Development and Psychopathology, 2,* 61–69.

Wainwright-Sharp, J. A., & Bryson, S. E. (1993). Visual orienting deficits in high-functioning people with autism. *Journal of Autism and Developmental Disorders, 23*(1).

Williams, D. (1992). *Nobody nowhere.* New York: Avon.

Williams, D. (1993). In S. Moreno (Ed.), *The Maap: A Newsletter For Families of More Advanced Autistic People, 4,* 6–10.

Williams, D. (1994). *Somebody somewhere.* New York: Avon.

Wing, L. (1992). Manifestations of social problems in high-functioning autistic people. In E. Schopler & G. B. Mesibov (Eds.), *High-functioning individuals with autism* (pp. 129–142). New York: Plenum.

Wulf, G. (1994). Sustained eye contact: One woman's victory. *Autism Network International Newsletter, 1*(3), 7.

Adolescence and Young Adulthood

Ann Fullerton

2

Adolescence is a period in which we separate from childhood attachments and roles and acquire adult ones instead (Blos, 1979). The upheavals and intensity of these years are testimony to how difficult this transition is for all of us. During the teen years we lose our childhood view of our parents as all-nurturing or all-powerful protectors. The loss of this view leaves a void, and adolescents can feel stranded and defenseless until they form their own adult identities. As a result, teenagers can experience intense vulnerability, isolation, and loss (Wexler, 1991). In response, teens often develop an intense attachment to their peer group. They also begin the work of building a new self-identity and in the process become very self-focused for a period of time. Lastly, teens begin to find their sense of direction for adult life, trying on various adult roles and worldviews (Ingersoll, 1989).

This rocky road is the *normal* course of adolescence, shared by higher functioning students with autism and their peers alike. In this chapter firsthand accounts and insights from parents and teachers are used to explore two aspects of adolescence: peer relationships and the development of a new self-awareness and self-identity. The goal of this chapter is to reflect on what young persons with autism *and their peers* are experiencing.

PEER RELATIONSHIPS

Peer relationships reach their height of importance during early and middle adolescence.

Although adults sometimes view teens' intense ties to their peer group as negative, the peer group serves an important role in the transition to adult social roles. It provides a protective setting in which to establish independence from parents and begin to formulate one's own values (Johnson, 1981). In time, however, the teen establishes independence from the peer group as well, as early love relationships are formed. These set the stage for later intimate and adult relationships (Selman, 1980). It is in the midst of these new peer relationships and social interactions that teens develop new levels of social knowledge, perspective taking, social awareness, and social competence.

One's ability to see another person's perspective is a socio-cognitive ability that develops over time. Young children are not aware that others have perspectives and thoughts that are different from their own. In the early elementary years, children are able to understand that others view a physical object differently, but they have little awareness that others also view situations and experiences differently.

Later, during older childhood and early adolescence, one gradually realizes that others *do* have their own thoughts and feelings. At first, however, one assumes that the feelings and values of others are the same as one's own. This perception is the basis for teens' certainty that any doubts or criticisms they have about themselves are shared by an invisible audience of others. Particular activities or possessions become all-important to the teen at this stage because "everybody's doing it" or "everybody has one" (Elkind, 1978).

In older childhood one also begins to think of one's relationships with friends as extending beyond immediate needs, as valuable for the sake of the relationship itself. Friendship behavior becomes reciprocal; friends take turns, they make deals, they depend on a sense of fair play, and they can see the friendship extending into the future (Selman, 1980).

Then, in middle and late adolescence, reciprocity evolves into mutual collaboration (Selman, 1980). Older teens are able to reconcile their needs and the needs of others. The adolescents recognize not only that they have multiple emotions, but also that others also have multiple emotions and that those emotions may differ from their own. This new insight is often learned in the context of a friendship (Selman, 1980).

Along with the experiences and insights gained through peers, by young adulthood the individual has also experienced a variety of other social contexts with adults (e.g., work). Thus, the young adult becomes increasingly aware of the complex nature of social interactions and social roles (Selman, 1980).

By young adulthood our social competence, or ability to analyze and respond to complex social settings, has matured to an amazing level (Eisenberg & Harris, 1984). There are several social cognitive skills that people possess and use in social situations:

> First, the individual's social competence is dependent upon the ability to decode the setting. That is, the individual must be able to accurately identify the critical cues in a social setting. Second, the individual must decide which, from among many alternative behaviors, is the most effective and appropriate response. Third, the individual must translate that decision into an actual, smooth behavior. At the same time, the individual receives subtle feedback from others in the social setting to indicate how adequate or appropriate their response was. Lastly, the individual must be able to recognize and interpret this feedback correctly and then know how to adjust their behavior in reponse to the

feedback. . . . (Dodge et al., 1986, quoted in Ingersoll, 1989, p. 245)

STUDENTS WITH AUTISM'S EXPERIENCES WITH PEERS

It is important to fully appreciate the importance of peer relationships and the social maturation that occurs during adolescence because it can help us understand

- what students with autism's peers are experiencing.

- what students with autism are experiencing.

- what students with autism are trying to understand and become a part of.

- why students with autism may experience an increasing gap between themselves and their peers during the adolescent years.

Within the new friendships and peer groups of the teen years, the format and context for social interaction change. The format for social interaction includes the words, gestures, and body language of social interchange. The context for social interaction is what people are "doing" together or the hidden rules that govern a social setting.

In late childhood the format and context for social interaction are fairly clear and concrete. Kids play games, engage in activities, "do stuff" together. But in adolescence the format and context for social interaction becomes much more vague and abstract (Figure 2.1). Teens spend more time sitting or standing around and talking, "hanging out," watching "what's happening." When these unspoken rules for how to interact become more subtle and unobservable, the teen with autism may have a difficult time knowing that the rules have changed and understanding the new rules.

In addition, the language used in conversation among teenagers becomes more sophisticated. The use of slang increases, and students start to understand and use sarcasm and cynicism. Teenagers with autism may miscommunicate with their peers because they take the phrases

FIGURE 2.1. During adolescence the context of social interaction changes.

they hear their peers use and try to use them literally or in the wrong context. This can lead to being teased and rejected.

Teenage peer groups are by nature clannish. Individual teens are often insecure about their acceptance within the group and worried that they are not just like their peers and thus won't "belong." At the same time, teens' cognitive and language abilities are rapidly developing and they seek opportunities to try them out. Thus individual teens may ostracize outsiders who are different in sophisticated and subtle ways in an effort to impress their group. They may be too vulnerable themselves to be willing to associate with someone who is different.

As teens form more sophisticated relationships, they attain a new level of social contextual knowledge and awareness of social cues. Such social competence is the specific area that the student with autism finds most challenging. Miscommunications with peers may occur right at the time that the teen with autism has become keenly interested in new kinds of social relationships. As a result, these miscommunications are especially painful. In this manner, the gap between students with autism and their peers can widen.

Several examples of misinterpretations both by students with autism and by their peers during the teen years are provided below. These examples illustrate what can happen in a high school setting but do not, however, help one anticipate a specific situation. How a particular student with autism will view a social situation and how peers will react will be unique to those involved.

These examples are best understood from two standpoints: first, that the student with autism is actively trying to interpret a situation and take part in it based on that interpretation, and second, that teachers must step back and try to figure out how the student with autism is interpreting a situation in order to understand the student's behavior (see Chapter 5).

▶ EXAMPLE 1:

Peers misinterpret a student with autism's strategies for coping with the noise and movement in the school hallways (Figure 2.2).

Susan Moreno (1991), the mother of a higher functioning woman with autism, describes a conversation she had with her daughter's high school classmates. Susan was explaining to the group that her daughter Beth needed friendship.

One of the peers commented, "You tell us that she wants our friendship, but when I say 'Hi!' to her in the halls, she doesn't even look up or answer me. I don't call that very friendly. I think *you* just want her to have friends." I quickly explained that my daughter wasn't replying to this girl in the halls because of the noise and fast movement around her, making the halls a very difficult and even frightening place. My daughter probably didn't see or hear the girl because she was focused on navigating the hall to get to her next class. This explanation was accepted with a little skepticism and then a lot of relief by the peer. (Moreno, 1991, p. 10)

▶ EXAMPLE 2:

Students with autism observe friendships among their peers, form their own definition of friendship based on what they see, and then act on it.

What is a friend? When one sees two people interacting, one may infer that the two people are friends based on how they respond to each other. But one does not know with absolute certainty that the two people are friends. One knows that there exist private aspects of the relationship one cannot see. It is this hidden aspect that determines whether the two people see each other as friends or not.

Students with autism may adopt a fairly concrete definition of friendship based on actions they can see. For example, the student with autism might think something like, "Friends are two people who sit and talk together several times a week at school. Friends also have lunch together in the cafeteria and do things on the weekend." Although these activities may be an important part of a friendship, they do not in and of themselves define a series of interactions as growing into a friendship.

However, if students with autism have different definitions of friendship, then they may misinterpret the actions of their peers. Thus, when peers have lunch with them once or twice at school, the students with autism may consider them to be their friends. When the students with autism then ask the peers to do more activities together than the peers are ready to, the peers may avoid them.

It is at this point that students with autism may become confused. In their minds, the peers were their friends and thus they continue to act upon that assumption. But based on an incomplete understanding of the subtleties of how friendships develop, students with autism may persist and not recognize social cues such as

FIGURE 2.2. High school hallways may be difficult to navigate.

the peers signaling that they are not interested in friendship at this time.

▶ EXAMPLE 3:

> *The student with autism is not aware of non-verbal social cues used by a clique that send a message to others on the school grounds that "this is our space"* (Figure 2.3).

Imagine for a moment that a social scientist from another planet is looking down from a space ship and observing the school grounds of an elementary, middle, and high school. In all three settings the scientist observes students by themselves and in groups. Without knowledge of the unwritten social rules in operation at these three different stages of development, the scientist may see the three situations as essentially the same.

It can be difficult for a student with autism to also recognize that the rules have changed as they and their peers move into early and late adolescence. Whereas in grade school it was okay to walk up and join various games going on, in junior high and even more so in high school, the rules have changed. At these ages, when a clique of students are standing around one does not walk up and join them or walk through their loosely formed circle. If it's a gang, one does not even walk too near their "turf." To do so might be interpreted as a challenge.

To further complicate matters, this rule might apply to some groups one encounters but not to others. For example, it's okay to join the meetings of the computer club at any time. Thus, one also has to know the nature of a group's association and purpose. High school students with autism can have difficulty recognizing a group's signals and learning these unwritten rules.

▶ EXAMPLE 4:

> *Students with autism attempt to emulate peers they admire but misinterpret the reason for their peers' behaviors and do not know when to engage in the behavior.*

A high school student with autism saw girls whom she admired wearing different outfits. She thought that they were changing their outfits several times during the day. She told her mother she needed to have two or three outfits for each day of school. Her family had recently emigrated, and the mother was not aware that this was not customary, so she helped her daughter prepare and pack the clothes for each day.

Teachers became aware of what the student was doing when she was late for class because she was trying to change her outfit between classes. The student had been doing this with great effort for several weeks. It was hard for the student to explain why she was doing this; in her mind she thought she was being like her peers. But like any teenager, she was reluctant to discuss this with adults. She just wanted to be left alone to continue to do what was by now in her mind very important for her success with her peers.

Another female student noticed that male students were socially included and accepted by other male students when they told jokes with sexual content. She began telling such jokes herself but did so at the wrong time, such as in mixed groups of boys and girls and when adults were present. She did not recognize that her peers engaged in "locker room" talk only with particular same-sex friends and only when adults were absent. As a result, she was laughed at by her peers. Because she didn't understand *why* they were laughing, she continued to tell jokes at the wrong time and to the wrong people.

FIGURE 2.3. It may be difficult to recognize the nonverbal social cues of groups.

These examples are very different, but they have in common the fact that the young adults with autism are trying to make sense of the social world of their peers. Teens with autism have difficulty recognizing the social cues and learning the unwritten social rules that govern their peers' behaviors.

In discussing friendship, one young woman said, "I'd like people to be my friend. Other adults have lost their innocence, but I still have mine. If they will give me their sophistication, I will give them back their innocence. I have something to offer as a friend" (personal communication, 1993).

EMOTIONS, STRESS, AND ANXIETY DURING ADOLESCENCE

The emotional upheavals of adolescence can be very difficult for the young person with autism. The young adult with autism may have to cope with the changes adolescence brings without the opportunities for peer group discussion and support utilized by others at this life stage (Dewey & Everard, 1974). With increased awareness of one's differences in social situations and repeated lack of success in forming friendships, a young person can be vulnerable to depression (Wing, 1981, 1992). Some persons will clearly express their sadness. But depression may manifest itself in ways that are hard to detect, such as a decreased desire for social contact and increased adherence to certain routines and solitary interests (Wing, 1981, 1992).

Many persons with autism report that social situations can be very stressful and confusing. Because of their intellectual strengths, more is expected of higher functioning persons with autism than persons with more obvious challenges (Wing, 1992). The effort to avoid doing the wrong thing in social situations, particularly when one is not sure what the wrong thing would be, can be highly stressful. For example, one young man explained that "as a general rule, the more 'normal' [my] behavior appears, the more guarded and anxious [I am] . . ." (Cesaroni & Garber, 1991, p. 309).

In addition to such situational anxiety, some persons with autism experience a physiologically based, constant, exhausting anxiety (Bemporad, 1979; Rumsey, Duara, Grady, Rapoport, Margolin, Rapoport, & Cutler, 1985; Grandin, 1992). Temple Grandin experienced this with the onset of puberty. Temple said that it "was like a constant feeling of stage fright. . . . Just imagine how you felt when you did something really anxiety provoking, such as your first public speak-

ing engagement. Now just imagine if you felt that way most of the time for no reason. . . . It was like my brain was running at 200 miles an hour, instead of 60 miles an hour . . ." (Grandin, 1992, p. 111).

As noted in Chapter 1, Temple's anxiety led her to invent a "squeeze machine" at age 18. The machine allows its users to control the amount of pressure they apply to the sides of the body by pulling on a lever. For Temple and others, the deep pressure provided by the squeeze machine can be very calming. Grandin (1992) and others also report that strenuous exercise can reduce anxiety. Other strategies Grandin has used are to fixate on an intense activity or to withdraw and try to minimize outside stimulation (Grandin, 1992).

For some persons, medication can also be beneficial in reducing anxiety. However, persons with autism can be extremely sensitive to the effects of medication, and it is critical that a physician knowledgeable about autism help determine the proper medication and dosage level (Grandin, 1992; McDonnell, 1993). Another useful strategy is to learn relaxation techniques. Groden and her associates (Cautela & Groden, 1978; Harrington, Samdperil, Groden, & Groden, 1991) have developed relaxation and imagery programs for persons with autism to use to reduce stress (see Resources at the end of this book). Many autism specialists agree that learning to use relaxation techniques and to recognize when one needs to use them is very important for many persons with autism.

Generally, autism specialists (Mesibov, 1992) and persons with autism themselves (Horner, 1993; Sinclair, 1992) do not find traditional psychotherapy aimed at gaining psychological insight to be effective for most persons with autism. Psychotherapy can even be deleterious if the persons with autism are made to feel that they are somehow at fault and not cooperating. Individual work with a therapist who is experienced with autism and that focuses on gaining understanding of social situations and events in the person's life can be very useful. Small groups of persons with autism that combine social support, practice in social situations, and explanations of social situations have also been helpful (Kilman & Negri-Shoultz, 1987; Mesibov, 1992).

DEVELOPING AN ADULT IDENTITY

The adolescent experiences such major physical and mental changes along with new social roles and demands that there is no way to avoid the question "Who am I?" As adolescents mature, their answers to this question become more multifaceted and include concrete as well as abstract descriptions (Montmayer & Eisen, 1977). Older children will describe themselves via what they do. Older adolescents will also describe what they think, feel, and value (Montemayor & Eisen, 1977). Developing self-awareness and then using it to develop a personal identity has been considered to be the single most important psychological turning point in our lives (Erikson, 1968). At some point during our adolescent years we put a moratorium on everything else and focus on this transformation of our identity; it takes a lot of work.

At the same time adolescents undergo a profound shift in their ability to think about the world (Inhelder & Piaget, 1958). Rather than being tied to concrete reality, the adolescents' conceptual world expands to encompass abstract reality and abstract possibility (Ingersoll, 1989) (see Figure 2.4). They are able to use increasingly sophisticated and efficient strategies to solve problems because they can now formulate and test out a hypothesis. Whereas the child is incapable of handling ambiguities or exceptions to the rules, the adolescent may become fascinated by them (Ingersoll, 1989). They will argue solely for the sake of testing out the limits of their newfound cognitive abilities. Often as they acquire this new ability to think about what "might be," they go through a period of being highly idealistic and are frustrated with the restrictions adults place on the possibilities for social change (Ingersoll, 1989).

THE HIGHER FUNCTIONING ADOLESCENT WITH AUTISM

Higher functioning young adults with autism also grapple with forming an adult worldview and self-identity. Their cognitive capacity to think about more complex information is also increasing albeit in directions shaped by their cognitive style and strengths. If they have difficulty with time and social concepts, they can be confused about what becoming an adult means. For example, one high schooler became increasingly concerned with the implications of the expression "when you graduate, you'll be an adult and you will have to . . ." that was used by his teachers. He took this statement literally and couldn't understand how graduation would make him an adult when he had never had a date, didn't have his driver's license yet, etc. In his mind he wondered, "How can I be an adult when these things haven't happened yet?" In time, his teachers realized the source of his confusion (personal communication 1994).

Young adults with autism will use their own line of reasoning to form a worldview. For example, one young man was very interested in abstract questions such as "What is good art?" or "What could be said to all people that will make them stop all crime and violence?" His assumption was that there is a single best answer to these questions and if it could only be found, everyone would agree with it and act on it. In questioning people about such topics, he steered them toward applying percentages to the relative goodness of one art piece or of one solution to crime over another. His reasoning is that if people will quantify their comparisons, then the single best answer does exist and can be found. At this point in his life, this was one of the lines of thinking he used to construct his worldview. In discussing such matters one needs to respect and work with an individual's line of thinking.

FIGURE 2.4. Adolescents undergo a profound shift in their ability to think about the world (Ingersoll, 1989).

Many higher functioning persons with autism state that since childhood they have known they were different from others, but it was in adolescence that it became important to have a reason that they were different (Williams, 1992; McDonnell, 1993; personal communication, 1993–94). For these young adults, it followed that if the reason could be found, then it could be changed. Young adults with autism can be highly motivated toward increased self-knowledge. But like any of us, they seek reasons that make sense to them.

Young adults' emerging self-awareness can also take the form of realizing that others know something that they don't know. A personal goal may then become to ask others questions that will elicit from others answers in concrete and/or quantifiable terms that they can then put into practice (McDonnell, 1993; personal communication, 1993–94). Donna Williams states:

> What I wanted . . . were rules I could carry around with me that applied to all situations, regardless of context. I wanted rules without exceptions. It was like saying I would be able to tell right from left if we only did away with left. . . . (Williams, 1994, p. 65)

With their active, indeed proactive thinking, young adults may try to find the essence of what makes them different or what they are missing. Then it becomes important to them to have a formula or rules for how to be just like everyone else. For example, one young man had been told that his problem communicating was that he needed to use more inflection when he spoke. He hoped that if he could just learn to do that, he would be able to engage his peers in conversation better (personal communication, 1994).

Young adults may seek a concrete or quantifiable definition of an abstract social concept that they want to understand. When it is explained that the concept cannot be defined in this way, the young adults may respond by asking the question differently but with the same aim: to attain a concrete definition. Perhaps the young adults with autism have assumed that older, more knowledgeable persons do indeed have the answers. The young adults attempt to find the right line of questioning that will draw forth an explanation they can understand.

In assisting adolescents or young adults, one must provide them with guideposts that are concrete and descriptive while making it clear that these guidelines will not always apply and that they are likely to change. Providing "working" social rules is better than providing no information at all (Mesibov, 1992). But simplistic advice that is not based on an understanding of higher functioning autism is not helpful (Dewey, 1980). Margaret Dewey, the mother of a young man with autism, recalls that teachers scolded her son for not listening, but he only became increasingly nervous as he tried to avoid being scolded and thus found it even harder to comprehend. He was also told, "Stop being so self-centered." Dewey notes that her son talks from the viewpoint that is clear to him, his own. And "yet when he steps outside the boundaries of his own affairs and shows interests in the affairs of other people, he is likely to be called meddlesome" (Dewey, 1980, p. 1). This young man needed more information than just admonishments to change or stop something. One must make clear what is and is not relevant and carefully describe what is occurring in a social situation (Frith, 1989). Specific strategies for such social assistance are described in Chapter 5.

LEARNING FROM OTHERS WITH AUTISM

When young people begin to explore who they are and how autism affects them, it can be very useful to share with them the writings of other persons with autism. Temple Grandin (1986) and more recently Donna Williams (1992, 1994), Paul McDonnell (1993), Beth Moreno (1993), and Thomas McKean (1994) have written some of the first personal accounts. These authors are now being joined by many others through *Our Voice*, the newsletter of the Autism Network International (ANI), a self-advocacy organization (see Resources). Through ANI's newsletter and telecommunications network, members share their insights and strategies in letters and dialogue. Another excellent source of ideas from higher functioning persons with autism and their family members is the MAAP (More-Able Autistic Persons) newsletter published by Sue Moreno (see Resources).

In reviewing the writings of higher functioning persons with autism, one can find much that is unique. There is also a recurring theme in recent issues of the ANI newsletter (1992–1994) around building an identity as a person with autism. The challenge discussed is that of being true to oneself (one's preferences, one's needs, one's ways of doing things) and at the same time trying to be a part of the social world. In the following list, thoughts from various writers have been summarized:

- Autism is a pervasive and integral part of who I am. My insights into myself and the world are the most valid ones for me (Baird & Blackmore, 1994).

- My way of sensing and perceiving the world and my way of thinking about the world are of value to myself and to others (Baird & Blackmore, 1994).

- Whatever others want to tell me, I am going to have to understand in my own terms and form my own meanings (Sinclair, 1992).

- I want information, but I don't want to be changed or cured or fixed. I want to learn from others and they can learn from me, but I don't want to try to change everything about me (nor can I) in order to be with you. You need to meet me halfway (Baird & Blackmore, 1994).

- I choose to moderate and control the amount of input I receive and the social situations I am in. I can't (nor do I care to) meet all of your social expectations (Horner, 1993).

- "Even if an autistic person has the same goals as a nonautistic person he or she might need to follow a different procedure to get there . . . " (Sinclair, 1992, p. 15).

RESPECTING ADOLESCENTS' AND YOUNG ADULTS' SELF-INSIGHTS

By the time persons with autism reach adolescence, they have developed strategies for coping with their sensory, cognitive, and social challenges. It is very important to listen to what young persons with autism know about their own needs and to help them build that knowledge into personal strategies and life pursuits that work for them.

In talking to young adults about their experience in high school, one discovers that sometimes their solutions to problems they faced were not considered by others. For example, one young woman (personal commmunication, 1993) was a member of the track team and loved to run. She asked that her high school schedule be arranged so that she could take Physical Education fourth period and run to calm herself down at mid-day. She knew this would make it possible for her to get through the rest of the school day. But her request was seen as being too rigid and asking for special privileges. She knew what she needed but she did not have the communicative ability to defend her reasons and persuade the adults involved.

CHAPTER SUMMARY

In this chapter the challenges of adolescence for both higher functioning students with autism and their peers were examined. The impact of new cognitive abilities, peer relationships, and the struggle to form an adult identity were discussed. Examples from the lives of young persons with autism were used to highlight these challenges. The background information given in this chapter is important for understanding the various teaching strategies provided in the remainder of this guide.

REFERENCES

Baird, C., & Blackmore, G. (1994). Hominids socializing. *Our Voice: The Newsletter of the Autism International Network, 4,* 20–26.

Bemporad, J. R. (1979). Adult recollections of a formerly autistic child. *Journal of Autism and Developmental Disorders, 9,* 179–197.

Blos, P. (1979). *The adolescent passage.* New York: International Universities Press.

Cautela, J. R., & Groden, J. (1978). *Relaxation: A comprehensive manual for adults, children, and children with special needs.* Champaign, IL: Research Press.

Cesaroni, L., & Garber, M. (1991). Exploring the experience of autism through firsthand accounts. *Journal of Autism and Developmental Disorders, 21*(3), 303–313.

Dewey, M. A. (1980). *The socially aware autistic adult and child.* Talk given at the Warwick Conference, Nottingham University, England.

Dewey, M., & Everard, M. (1974). The near normal autistic adolescent. *Journal of autism and childhood schizophrenia, 4,* 348–356.

Dodge, K. A., Pettit, G. S., McClaskey, C. L., & Brown, M. M. (1986). Social competence in children. *Monographs for the Society for Research in Child Development, 51* (2, Serial No. 213).

Eisenberg, N., & Harris, J. D. (1984). Social competence: A developmental perspective. *School Psychology Review, 13,* 278–291.

Elkind, D. (1978). Understanding the young adolescent. *Adolescence, 49,* 127–134.

Erikson, E. (1968). *Identity, youth, and crisis.* New York: Norton.

Frith, U. (1989). *Autism: Explaining the enigma.* Oxford: Blackwell Press.

Grandin, T. (1992). An inside view of autism. In E. Schopler & G. B. Mesibov (Eds.), *High-functioning individuals with autism* (pp. 105–126). New York: Plenum.

Harrington, B., & Samdperil, D. L. (Producers), & Groden, G., & Groden, J. (Directors). (1991). *Breaking the barriers II* (Videotape). The Groden Center Inc., Rhode Island.

Horner, L. (1993). Some things which work and some things which don't and why I'm happy being autistic. *Our Voice: The Newsletter of the Autism International Network, 2,* 19–23.

Ingersoll, G. M. (1989). *Adolescents* (2). Englewood Cliffs, NJ: Prentice-Hall.

Inhelder, B., & Piaget, J. (1958). *The growth of logical thinking from childhood to adolescence.* New York: Basic Books.

Johnson, D. W. (1981). Social psychology. In F. Farley & N. Gordon (Eds), *Psychology and education: The state of the union.* Berkeley, CA: McCutcheon.

Kilman, B., & Negri-Shoultz, N. (1987). Developing educational programs for working with students with Kanner's autism. In D. J. Cohen, A. M. Donnellan, & R. Paul (Eds.), *Handbook of autism and pervasive developmental disorders* (pp. 440–451). Silver Spring, MD: V. H. Winston & Sons.

McDonnell, P. (1993). Paul's story (afterword). In J. T. McDonnell (Ed.), *News from the border: A mother's memoir of her autistic son* (pp. 327–376). New York: Ticknor & Fields.

McKean, T. (1994). *Soon will come the light.* Arlington, TX: Future Education, Inc.

Mesibov, G. B. (1992). Treatment issues with high-functioning adolescents and adults with autism. In E. Schopler & G. B. Mesibov (Eds.), *High-functioning individuals with autism* (pp. 143–155). New York: Plenum.

Montemayor, R., & Eisen, M. (1977). The development of self-conceptions from childhood to adolescence. *Developmental Psychology, 13,* 314–319.

Moreno, B. (1993). My side of the story. Available from the More Able Autistic Persons (MAAP) Newsletter, Susan Moreno (Ed.). P.O. Box 524, Crown Point, IN 46307.

Moreno, S. J. (1991). *High-functioning individuals with autism: Advice and information for parents and others who care.* Maap Services, Inc., P.O. Box 524, Crown Point, IN 46307.

Rumsey, J. M., Duara, R., Grady, C., Rapoport, J. L., Margolin, R. A., Rapoport, S. L. & Cutler, N. R. (1985). Brain metabolism in autism. *Archives of General Psychiatry, 42,* 448–455.

Selman, R. L. (1980). *The growth of interpersonal understanding: Developmental and clinical analyses.* New York: Academic Press.

Sinclair, J. (1992). Editorial: What does being different mean? *Our Voice: The Newsletter of the Autism International Network 1,* 14–16.

Wexler, D. B. (1991). *The adolescent self: Strategies for self-management, self-soothing, and self-esteem in adolescents.* New York: W. W. Norton.

Williams, D. (1994). *Somebody somewhere. Breaking free from the world of autism.* New York: Avon.

Williams, D. (1992). *Nobody nowhere: The extraordinary autobiography of an autistic.* New York: Avon.

Wing, L. (1981). Asperger's syndrome: A clinical account. *Psychological Medicine, 11,* 115–129.

Wing, L. (1992). Manifestations of social problems in high-functioning autistic people. In E. Schopler & G. B. Mesibov (Eds.), *High-functioning individuals with autism* (pp. 129–142). New York: Plenum.

Adapting Instructional Materials and Strategies

3

Joyce Stratton

In the current education system it is desirable for all students to participate in the regular instructional program as much as possible. This is true for students who are disabled as well as those who are not. Intended outcomes from this participation are a sense of belonging and the development of meaningful relationships with peers and significant adults. Students with autism share the desire to be a part of regular school life and, with carefully planned support, find this attainable.

In addition to social experiences, participation in educational instruction designed for typical middle or high school students is possible for the student with autism when appropriate modifications are used. Without support the student with autism is not able to gain as much from the instruction as teachers or parents desire. An element of educating students with autism that is challenging is the appearance of mastery or success without the ability to make practical application of information. The long-term outcome for students when instruction is not adapted for their learning style is a lack of ability to apply information to achieve competence or independence in their lives. The students continue to lack real skills to hold a job or take care of basic living problems.

This chapter will discuss the characteristics and learning style associated with autism as they apply to educating higher functioning students with autism. It will also develop methods by which individual students may be assessed to understand the impact of autism on their ability to benefit from instruction. Finally, the chapter lists modifications, adaptations, and interventions that are appropriate for the student with autism as support in an education setting.

COGNITIVE CHARACTERISTICS IN AUTISM

Problems in the instructional process originate with the impact that autism has on learning. The teacher or parent will desire to understand this impact in order to make decisions about the support and assistance a student needs. Understanding begins with a look at the core attribute common to all persons with autism. Frith describes this attribute as "the inability to draw together information so as to derive coherent and meaningful ideas. There is a fault in the predisposition of the mind to make sense of the world" (Frith, 1989, pp. 186–187). The effect of this information processing problem results in the unique characteristics associated with autism.

The particular characteristics that impact cognitive functioning are central to the learning style employed by students with autism. The cognitive characteristics typical in autism are caused by problems with information processing. How the brain takes in, stores, and uses information is different from the norm. Information becomes confused and segregated in the brain. It is a problem of seeing the world from unusual perspectives. The cognitive characteristics are present to some degree in all persons with autism, but the severity and impact of the characteristics on the learning process will vary with the individual (Frith, 1989).

Cause-and-Effect Relationships

Difficulty understanding cause-and-effect relationships is one of the cognitive deficits. For the student with autism, an event is not necessarily associated with the effect it causes. Similarly, a sequence of events may not seem related to each other. Events may be perceived as distinct and separate from each other. As a result, inferences and conclusions are difficult or impossible to draw (Frith, 1989).

Focus on Details

Another cognitive characteristic is a tendency to focus on irrelevant or insignificant details and miss the central meaning in a situation. At times the persons with autism may focus on a narrow interest of their own to the exclusion of almost everything else. At other times they may select erroneous information as significant or experience faulty interpretation.

Certain environmental events can be sufficiently distracting to make it difficult to focus on what is important. A great deal of noise or certain types of noise can be difficult for some students. Other students may be disrupted by students moving around during class as well as windows or other visual information on the walls. Most students with autism are distracted by something, and this may vary considerably from student to student (Mesibov, 1990–91).

Sequencing

Students with autism do not sequence and organize in the same manner as students without autism (Mesibov, 1990–91). One common form of compensation is for information to be stored in memory in a rote manner. Retrieving information or "breaking into" the sequence in the middle can be very difficult at times. An example concerning Temple Grandin, the noted author with autism described in earlier chapters, is an inability to give directions unless she can start from the beginning with no interruptions. If the listener asks a question or interrupts, she must start over from the beginning (Sacks, 1993/1994).

The sequencing problem has many other results. The ability to put events or information together logically is impaired. The ability to organize oneself is limited. The student may need frequent assistance in knowing where to start a task or when it is finished (Janzen, 1992b).

Understanding of Time

Concepts of time are abstract and difficult to understand for the student with autism. Most people perceive the passage of time through a complex system of internal and external signals. For the person with autism, there is an inadequate ability to comprehend the signals that determine the passage of time without the aid of specifics such as a watch. The result is an overfocus on watches or schedules. Often the high functioning student with autism is the first one in kindergarten to have mastered time telling. The overfocus also shows up in asking many repetitive time or schedule-related questions throughout the day (Janzen, 1989).

It is important to allow the student access to a schedule at all times. Many teachers and parents often feel their students with autism have an excellent ability to remember their schedules because of the ability to recite it. Extreme caution on the part of teachers and parents will help the comfort of the students in this area, however. Students with autism work very hard to compensate for the deficits they experience in this area and need written and visual supports on an ongoing basis throughout their lives.

Compulsiveness

Compulsions and obsessions are traits of autism that are often noted by teachers and particularly parents. At times compulsive routines are difficult to manage or interrupt. Often there is a compulsive perfectionism and a strong sense of right and wrong. This may produce intense feelings if things are done incorrectly and ongoing fear that this will happen. A result may be a reluctance to try new things. At times this can take the form of acting out or resistance. A complication to this problem arises when persons with autism do not ask for help sufficiently well to let you know they are having a problem (Janzen, 1992a).

Distractibility

Distractibility is a major problem over which students with autism have little control. Environmental distractions such as extraneous noises are difficult. Screening out information that is not needed often has to be a conscious process and even then may not achieve the desired results. An example again comes from Temple Grandin, who describes an inability to use a telephone in an airport because attempts to shut out the background noise also cut out the sounds coming through the telephone (Grandin, 1988).

Cognitive distractibility can be a problem for higher functioning students with autism as well. This process occurs when thoughts that most people can lay aside become a focus when trying to do other things. This can occur easily if there has been an incident that is stressful or upsetting to the individuals. They will find it difficult to stop thinking about it until they experience some type of closure first.

Confusion

The overall result of the cognitive characteristics of autism is tremendous confusion. This confusion is often masked by overall anxiety and stress. Stress can be expressed in typical ways such as general nervousness. However, increases in stress are often expressed and shown in unusual ways such as the behaviors typically identified with autism. As a result, this anxiety is often not easily recognized as a stress response. Stress responses can take the form of stereotypical behaviors, repetitive questioning, acting out, withdrawal, or acting silly. One response to confusion commonly seen is "getting stuck"—a task or routine is not started or may be stopped before it is completed.

LEARNING STYLE ASSOCIATED WITH AUTISM

The learning style of a student with autism is a product of the cognitive characteristics. Learning style traits may be thought of as symptoms of autism but are not the core underlying problem. Because the learning style traits are symptoms, it is helpful for the teacher or parent to remember the cause of that symptom. Assistance or intervention for the student when the teacher or parent responds to the underlying, core processing problem rather than just the symptoms achieves more success. With autism the understanding of "why" is as important to effective teaching as the "how."

Learning Rate and Ability

An ability to learn quickly is a trait common to persons with autism. Rote, factual, and favorite topic information can be learned very fast. Once learned, however, information can be difficult to change.

Another learning trait is an inability to draw from incidental or inferential teaching in which self-discovery is the method used (Janzen, 1986). Learning in a self-discovery approach is only possible if the materials and experiences are enhanced and modified with explanations, visual structure, and visual information.

Students with autism generally learn best when using a visual mode to input information. Their memory for visual detail is usually quite good. In contrast, auditory memory is faulty and unreliable if the student must receive information just by listening (Janzen, 1986).

Language and Concepts

Language comprehension is a pervasive problem in students with autism, and it influences all learning. Abstract concepts usually need to be taught and are sometimes hard for the student to grasp (Frith, 1991). There is a tendency to not listen to directions carefully unless taught to do so. In addition, students often respond to verbal directions or information slowly and need a longer time to process and respond to what is said. There is often a need to repeat information out loud. This can be confused with echolalia at times, but it actually serves the purpose of allowing the student to rehearse information. This technique is most often used if it is new information or if the student is relearning a task in a new way.

Expression with language is also difficult. For example, it is not easy to tell others what they are doing, are supposed to be doing, or have done in a clear manner. This can be confusing to the teacher or parent because the student may appear to be verbal or in fact talk constantly. The deficit for the higher functioning students with autism is not the ability to talk but the ability to generate the important tools of communication to achieve effective interactions with others.

Impulse Control

Students with autism may have problems controlling impulses to do or say things at inappropriate times. The result in a classroom situation is that they speak out or move around more often than peers. They may also appear to have frequent outbursts that have an impulsive quality. In these situations what is actually occurring for the students is an inability to express frustration until they reach their limit of tolerance and have an outburst. This can make it appear that the outburst happens suddenly or quickly while it actually has been

building for some time. This problem is compounded by an inability to ask for help efficiently.

THE SIGNIFICANCE OF UNDERSTANDING THE CHARACTERISTICS OF AUTISM

Often teachers, parents, and others misinterpret the behavior of students with autism. The examples in Table 3.1 show how the behavior of a student may actually be a characteristic associated with autism even though it resembles behavior typically viewed as adolescent. For example, from time to time all high school teachers experience disinterest, disruptions, or defiance in their students. It can be easy to interpret the behavior of the student with autism from this frame of reference as well.

ASSESSMENT

Assessment is a key element in beginning effective instruction for students with autism (Mesibov, 1990–91). Assessment can occur on an informal or a formal basis. The questions that follow have been derived from lectures, training, and articles by Gary Mesibov and others at Division TEACCH in Chapel Hill, North Carolina. They are important to consider in all assessment activities. From this information will be determined what type and the extent of support a student will need for instruction and smooth functioning.

Learning Style and Impact of Autism

1. What are the strengths, weaknesses, and emerging skills of the student?

2. What are particular areas of interest or talent?

TABLE 3.1. Example of Teacher Misinterpretations

Student action	Teacher thinks the student	What is actually happening
Inattentiveness.	is daydreaming.	Student does not understand what to do and/or where to start.
Keeps asking the same question over and over.	is using attention-getting behavior.	Student is having difficulty understanding and may be confused.
Speaks out in class.	is using attention-getting behavior.	Student may not know which questions are meant for him or her or that other people may want to say something.
Calls others inappropriate names.	does not like contact with other students.	Student feels threatened from teasing or some other source of discomfort.
Never turns in homework.	will not do assigned work; is poorly motivated or stubborn.	Student does not know where to turn work in (so it never leaves the notebook).

3. Does the student understand cause-and-effect relationships (and first/then, work/break, safety, social correctness, etc.)?

4. What distractions are the most challenging to the student?

5. Does the student know when a task is finished without being told by others?

6. What does the student remember easily? What is difficult to remember?

7. How does the student like to know what is coming next?

8. Does the student adapt to new situations easily?

9. How does the student respond when he or she is wrong or needs to be corrected?

10. What does the student do when confused or anxious?

Approach to Tasks

1. How does the student start? Is there a pattern to the student's way of initiating a task?

2. How does the student process information (visual, auditory, kinesthetic)? How can you tell?

3. Does the student repeat directions out loud? If given written directions will the student use them effectively in the task?

4. Does the student wait and attend to directions or immediately start on a task without directions? Conversely, does the student seem to be too dependent on directions to start a task?

5. Does the student change his or her approach to a task if the task changes or needs modifications? How? Does the student often revert to the former answer even if it is no longer valid for the task?

6. Does the student need a model or example of the task to look at to fully understand what he or she is doing and to increase competency?

7. Does the student work through a task or project with only one direction, or is a series of directions needed to keep the student going? Is the student's work smoother if the directions are in a visual form?

8. Does the student ask for help or know when he or she has a problem? How does the student express this?

9. What nonverbal signs are present when the student is having a difficult time or need help?

10. Is the student able to tell when he or she made a mistake and correct the errors independently? Does the student experience a great deal of frustration if he or she makes a mistake or is asked to correct the work?

FUNCTIONAL ACADEMIC SKILLS

Functional academics should be included in educational programs for a student with autism. An assessment of daily living skills may be conducted for educational planning as well as determining long-term support needs. Many assessment tools are available from commercial publishers. One assessment that is very comprehensive is the "Home Life Checklist" by Nancy Dalrymple (1987), from the Indiana Resource Center in Bloomington, Indiana.

Daily living skill assessments should include all factors for independent living, such as safety with medications, ability to take care of health needs (including visiting a doctor independently), and ability with money. Listed in Table 3.2 are other areas of functional skills that should be considered for students with autism that may not be found on standard assessments.

TABLE 3.2. Functional Skills

SKILL AREA	EXAMPLES
Reading	
Understanding the purpose of and ability to use:	Discriminating valid from junk mail, such as credit card applications, contests, and others with misleading ads so as to respond appropriately
• newspapers	
• community bulletins	
• community posters	
• menus	
• bus schedules	
• city maps	
• TV guides	
• phone book	
Directions for games or electronic equipment	Interest stories
Directions for model kit assembly	Comic books
Reference materials and resources	Magazines

(continues)

TABLE 3.2. *Continued*

SKILL AREA	EXAMPLES
Functional geography	Work-related information such as company policies or rules
Personal Management	
Following recipes	Following survival signs
Reading directions on labels	Planning balanced meals
Properly administering medication—over-the-counter and prescription	Following directions on home appliances such as microwaves, dishwashers, washers, dryers
Computers	
Playing games	Budgeting and banking
Reading directions to access programs	Word processing
Uses of Internet	Electronic mail
Writing	
Personal letters	Job application
Personal schedule and "To Do" list	Research papers: application and synthesis of materials
Daily diary or journal	Taking messages for others
Address and phone book	Taking notes for own use
Math	
Budgeting	Functional use of money
Measurements	Fractions for everyday use
Time and calendars	Calculator use

ASSISTANCE

There are two levels of assistance in the education of students with disabilities:

- Level 1: *Modifications and adaptations* are the easiest and least intrusive methods of assistance.
- Level 2: *Intervention and direct assistance* require more direct help from an instructor and may require more time.

For the student with autism, ongoing methods of assistance and help from both levels allow compensation for the impact of autism on the educational process. It is vital to the success of the student that these are ongoing and available throughout the day. The strategies developed for assistance should not be removed even if the student appears to be proficient in that area. They are usually experiencing success because of the modification, and without it their learning and independence will be diminished.

Another aspect of support that is very important to independence is the manner in which support is provided. Support should be independent of an instructor's verbal and physical presence. It should instead be incorporated into the environment and teaching methods or materials. Several methods of support that are provided in this way are shown in Table 3.3 for both Level 1 and Level 2.

Modifications and Adaptations

Most modifications and adaptations occur as a part of the regular instruction or student management process. They are added to the usual routine as a support, much as a person with a broken leg uses crutches to walk independent of assistance from others. At times more assistance is required, but careful assessment of the circumstances and student needs will deter-mine the amount, duration, and type. The modifications and adaptations listed here will provide support for the student with autism. This list could be much longer, and many variations are possible. This is an area where assessment, intuition, and teamwork are vital for developing the best possible strategies for each unique individual. The goal of assistance is always to allow the student to be as independent from direct adult supervision and ongoing direction as possible.

Time Management and Schedules. One area of support that is vital to the success of the student with autism that is not addressed in this chapter is time management and scheduling. These issues are addressed in Chapter 4, which is an important companion to the information in this chapter. Time management strategies and personal schedules are always necessary for the student with autism.

TABLE 3.3. Level of Support

Student Need	Level 1: Modifications and Adaptations	Level 2: Intervention and Direct Assistance
Following directions	Visual instructions	Visual notes
Language comprehension	Semantic organizers or visuals for key points	Concept and vocabulary development
Assignments	Reduced workload and clear directions	
Involvement in class groups	Small-group goals and pregroup work	
Grades	Goal grading, extra credit, prearrange-ments, advance warnings	Pass/no pass or teacher/student conferences
Homework	Complete instructions and parent involvement	Concept development
Essay work	Specific directions	Outline development
Tests and exams	Oral or written tests, distraction-free environments	
Class discussions	Redirections	Advance organizers
Stress	Breaks and stress-reduction plans	Asking for help with visual prompts

Following Directions: Visual Instructions. Provide visual information about tasks and projects in order to increase the student's understanding and efficiency in following directions. Words, photographs, pictographs (simple line drawings), or combinations of these may be used to supply the visual information.

Instructions should include the entire task, activity, or sequence of activities (see the example in Figure 3.1). A series of directions or steps to complete the task should provide the most comprehensive details. Information about the finished product should be included (Janzen, 1989).

Other components of instructions include

- how much work they are to do.
- where to begin.
- what to do and in what order.
- when it is finished.
- what the finished product looks like.
- what to do next.

This information must be presented in an organized, visual manner understandable to the student.

Language Comprehension. To take advantage of the visual strengths of students with autism, all class lectures, directions, and explanations should be represented visually as well as verbally. Information that must be used or remembered only from hearing it is generally unreliable and misinterpreted more often than if the visual channel is also used. Some traditional methods of assistance such as reading along in a text is often not the type of visual help needed because of possible reading comprehension and vocabulary problems. Other visual supports are often needed to provide a clear, meaningful picture to the student.

Semantic Organizers. A method of visually representing material is semantic organizers or story maps, topic mapping, or webbing. In this method the main points of the information are arranged in a logical manner or sequence and connected by lines to help show their relationships to each other. These can be drawn ahead of time, and the teacher can use a visual point to keep track on the topic map as he or she talks. A more effective use of the semantic organizer is to draw it as the material is being presented (Pefiesson, 1989). An example of a semantic organizer is shown in Figure 3.2.

Group Work in Health Class

1. Write a 3-page paper with 3 other kids in class.
2. Ms. Smith will tell you whom you will work with.
3. Your group will:
   - decide what your paper will be about.
   - meet for 30 minutes each day this week from 10:15 to 10:45.
   - write the paper on Friday and turn it in to the basket on my desk.
4. Check your goal card each day before you start.

FIGURE 3.1. Instructions should include the entire task or activity.

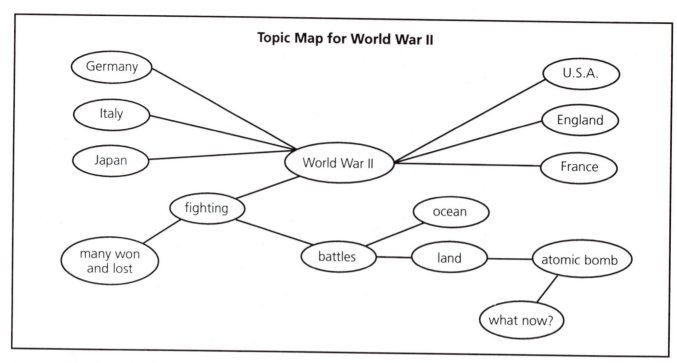

FIGURE 3.2. Example of semantic organizer.

Key Phrases or Main Points. Another strategy of visual assistance is to write out key words or phrases as a discussion or lecture takes place. This can be done with the entire class during regular instruction. An added benefit in the instructional process is found in increased attending by all students who are visual learers.

The key phrase strategy is also useful for another purpose for students with autism. Used in an individual manner, writing out a key word or phrase is helpful if the students are "stuck" due to frustration or confusion. They can be helped over the hurdle they are experiencing by giving them the essential information of what they are to do at that moment. A two-or three-word written direction at a time like this is highly effective. The "trick" to this strategy is identifying what or why the students are having a problem. The visual information given must be short, specific to the problem they are having, and written in a positive form.

Assignment Modifications: Reduced Work and Clear Directions. Because of the learning style of the student with autism, regular coursework assignments may require modification. Many students have difficulty completing assignments. The most common modification to help solve this problem is to require less work. Some types of coursework assume that students will need repetitive practice to learn and master a skill. The fast learning rate of students with autism allows them to master and retain a skill without this repetition. This is a good opportunity to reduce the amount of work required. At the same time the instructor can allow for possible writing problems many students with autism have.

In determining how much to modify the regular assignment, many factors should be taken into consideration. Areas to consider are students' writing ability, personal stamina, type of task and difficulty level for those students, knowledge of how fast the students learn, how they learn, what motivates the students, and how much work of that type they can do at one sitting and/or on their own. Take these factors into consideration and then test your assessment through careful observation of the students completing that work with the modification in place. If the students are able to successfully complete the work on their own, the optimum level has probably been reached. Be very cautious about giving more work the next time. For long-term support, assignment modifications that require less work will probably be a common practice rather than an occasional procedure.

When giving assignments always make the finished aspect of the task or project very clear. For effective time management teachers or parents should be able to match the amount of work to the time available based on their knowledge of the students. Modify the amount of work required so the students are able to complete it in the time allowed. Let the students know what to do with any finished products very specifically. Make sure they know when, how, and where to turn in assignments. Do not assume even the simplest thing. Students have been known to have their notebooks full of finished homework but never ask where they are supposed to turn it in.

Involvement in Class Groups: Small-Group Goals and Pregroup Work. In class settings the teacher may ask students to be involved in a variety of class groupings, from one large group to several small groups. Different types of support may be needed by students with autism when they are in various types of groups.

When the work is in small groups to complete tasks or projects, students with autism will be able to increase their contributions to the group if their roles are very clear to them. The teacher may give them a few specific goals (including a social goal) to meet during that group session. Put the goals in writing and give immediate feedback when the session is over about the success in meeting the goals. In small-group settings it can be very difficult for students with autism to contribute academic information and socially interact at the same time. To increase the amount of meaningful involvement, academic contributions can be developed prior to the group session so that the students already know what they will contribute and thus be able to concentrate on the social aspect. Figure 3.3 shows an example of written goals for a student while in a group that is developing a class presentation.

Modified Grading. Students with autism often have a difficult time with the concepts of grades. They may become overly anxious about their grades to the point that it affects their overall behavior. One student with autism became so upset because he was not achieving straight A's that he would not go to school. Other responses to grades may be total lack of understanding or general apathy. In both cases of over or under concern, the grades are essentially meaningless. Modifying the grading system can solve many problems and increase motivation and productivity in some situations.

Goal Grading. This strategy determines grades on the progress toward predetermined goals. The goals must be arrived at by the student, teacher, and parent to make sense to the

1. Tell your 3 ideas.
2. Say one thing about each idea.
3. Let the other group members talk about your idea.
4. Talk to everyone in the group at least one time. Remember to look at them.
5. It's OK if the group does not want to use your ideas.

FIGURE 3.3. A 3" × 5" goal card for the student to keep during group work.

student. They should be written down and reviewed with the student on a regular basis. A goal for English may be to write two essays of three pages each on selected topics. A goal for math may be to complete two pages a week in the math book and one page a week in a menu math workbook. The goals should be very specific and work oriented. If social- or work-related goals are to be included, they should be specific also. An example of a work-related goal may be to take notes during lectures using an outline worksheet or to check in with the teacher before class begins each day (Murphy, Meyers, Olesen, McKean, & Custer, 1988).

Extra Credit Opportunities. Opportunities are presented to students as an integral part of the program. These opportunities can draw on the individual students' strengths or particular areas of interest by allowing them to turn in work that uses those topics as a focus. For example, a student who has an intense interest in how money is coined and in metals may be able to write essays about this process as extra credit in English. Or the student may be able to write a letter to other coin collectors asking them for information for credit in writing or reading. In math, the student may be able to work out problems based on the chemical makeup of coins and the various proportions used. These assignments may also be used as substitution for other work that is difficult for the student (Murphy et al., 1988).

Prearrangements. Agreements as to the amount of work to be completed during each grading period can be effective for some students. The student and teacher agree, "If you do this much you get an A; for this much you can earn a B; and for this much you can earn a C." The agreement should be very specific. Parent involvement when forming these agreements is important (Murphy et al., 1988).

Advance Warning Systems. This system can be effective for students working within the usual grading systems. In this method two weeks before report cards are to be sent home,

the student is given a facsimile report card with the grade entered. If the student would like to improve the grade in the two weeks remaining, then alternatives or ways to bring the grade up to the desired level are arrived at by the teacher and student. This system must be made concrete for the student to be effective. Specific timelines for activities with frequent progress checks by the teacher and parents will be needed for success (Murphy et al., 1988).

Homework: Complete Instructions and Parent Involvement. Parents are a great asset to the educational team of a student with autism. Parents are generally very involved with their child and are committed to providing support to the school. In trying to provide support, one area that parents will often express frustration in is homework. Due to the communication difficulties of the student with autism, parents often do not have enough information to assist in homework effectively. To increase success with homework, the school staff may give complete directions directly to the parent. Make sure that parents can tell what the assignment is without having been in the class. Ask yourself, "If I had not been there, would I understand the directions for this assignment?" A general rule of thumb to consider for students with autism is to not rely on them to relay information home. It is not a matter of lack of responsibility but their problems with language and understanding that cause the information to get entirely forgotten or so distorted that the parents cannot get the message clearly (Moreno, 1991).

Essay Work: Specific Directions. Essay material assignments are often vague to students with autism because they are generally unaware of how much they are to write or whether they are really answering the question, part of the question, or their distorted understanding of the question. The language difficulties of autism become a major problem in these situations (Moreno, 1991). Giving clear written directions about how much to write, what to write, and how to know when they are finished will help clear up some of the confusion. Checking in with the students early in the work to provide feedback will help also.

Tests and Exams: Oral or Written Tests and Distraction-Free Environments. Test taking can be extremely stressful for students with autism. The problem of slow processing as well as the need to be perfect combine to make these situations often intolerable. Tests can be modified by using both an oral and a written version, changing the place to take tests, using a take-home test, or allowing other means to show that the material is learned and understood (Murphy et al., 1988). Give students ample opportunity to ask questions so that the teacher can be aware of how well the students are understanding what is being asked of them. It is easy to tell how well the students understand the test questions by whether their questions make sense to the teacher. At times a very small clarification can make a major difference to students with autism. They may be misunderstanding only one word in the question, but that is causing them to be unable to comprehend the entire question. By clarifying the one word, the teacher can enable the students to proceed independently.

An ongoing problem for students with autism is being able to ask for help when they need it. While taking tests or exams this problem may be worse because of stress the student may feel in the test-taking situation. A card with useful reminders can be a quick and easy strategy of assistance to the student (see Figure 3.4).

Class Discussions: Redirections. During discussion in large group settings, students with autism may be operating from an entirely different perspective than that of typical students. They may have a different perspective on why they are there, what is expected of them, or what the topic is. As a result, students may at times offer information that is on another topic than the one under discussion. These situations can easily appear humorous or bizarre to classmates. How the teacher responds to these comments will have a direct impact on the social success of the students with autism. If all students are treated with respect and care, the other students in class will often model the teacher's behavior toward the students with autism.

A few simple strategies can redirect students with autism back to the topic under discussion. When off-topic comments are made, relate them back to the body of the material with as logical a link-up as you can make. If the comment is so off topic that it is not possible to link it up, say, "Thank you, now can you tell me one thing about *(topic under discussion)*?" Avoid questions during discussion; use a "tell me" approach instead. In a "tell me" approach the teacher starts with "tell me about" and then leads into the topic or question. More information can be gained from students with autism through this approach than through usual questions. Always take any communication from students with autism seriously, and never laugh at them for an absurd-sounding comment. Examples of a "tell me" approach include the following.

- "Tell me about the work the President of the United States does."

- "Tell me about how the blood vessels help your body."

- "Tell me about _____."

- "Tell me what _____."

- "Tell me how _____."

---

1. Remember to ask for help if you are not sure about a word.
2. Remember to relax.

FIGURE 3.4. Exam cue card.

Stress: Breaks and Stress Reduction Plans. Teachers and parents can give significant help to students with autism by including methods of stress reduction in all routines and activities. One effective strategy is to offer a way for the student to withdraw from the class for a while if needed. A prearranged signal for a short break can avoid many problems or outbursts. When students come back from short breaks help them get into the flow of things quickly by telling them what just happened and what they are to do now. Arrange for a break area and allow a specific amount of time for breaks. It is helpful to remember when designing a system such as this that the students are rarely guilty of avoiding work but truly need a way to reduce the rigorous demands made on them because of their disability. If teachers or parents suspect that students are trying to avoid work, then the work must be analyzed as to whether the students understand it or whether a more effective form of motivation may be added.

If behavior outbursts occur avoid such questions as, "Why did you do that?" It is helpful to talk with students to determine what the problem is, but they may need a short break first before they are able to discuss the problem. An effective stress reduction program or plan can prevent outbursts if the plan is consistently used (Janzen, 1992a). Progressive relaxation techniques or imagery have proven successful in stress reduction for students with autism (Cautela & Groden, 1978; see also the Resources section at the end of this book).

Intervention and Direct Assistance

The second level of assistance consists of interventions and direct assistance that involve greater support. These strategies and methods often require more time from instructors than modifications and adaptations. Generally they require some direct involvement with an adult or possibly a peer for a specific purpose. This level of support is commonly needed by students when learning new material or learning about new environments. Some students may require increased intervention for certain activities while doing quite well with modifications or less support for much of their day. There is significant variance among students or even within one student's program as to the degree of intervention needed. This will vary with time and overall stress or anxiety level also. It is not a sign of regression if a student needs increased support at any given time.

Following Directions: Visual Notes. When a student has questions or problems, the teacher may give assistance in a visual manner by writing out directions and instructions and then leave the student. The teacher should check to see if the direction/instruction has been started correctly but should not stay any longer than necessary. The instruction will be the most effective if kept short and concrete.

Language Comprehension: Concept and Vocabulary Development. The language difficulties of students with autism are considered a major stumbling block to participation in many activities designed for the regular curriculum. The most difficult aspect for students with autism is understanding concepts or vocabulary if they have not had experience with it. Even with experience there is often incomplete understanding about that concept, which hinders effective understanding for the students (Frith, 1991).

With careful introduction and development of language concepts, the student with autism can gain a usable level of knowledge. When introducing new concepts or abstract vocabulary, the teacher or parent may start with the student's own experience or information about that concept. The next step is adding information that is similar but new to expand the student's understanding. Using semantic organizers during this process is very important to show the relationships between various pieces of information. An example might be a lesson in which the student is to learn about Russia. The teacher will start talking with the student about where the student lives. Next the state the student lives in is talked about. After that the United States is discussed with an emphasis that this is a country rather than a city or a state. At that point Russia can be introduced with the help of a map to show the two countries' geographic relationship. To teach about Russian culture or life, compare the student's life, the average life in the United States, and Russian life.

Grading: Pass/No Pass or Teacher-Student Conferences.

Alternatives to grades may be necessary for some students with autism. The basic program for those students may be so modified from the regular curriculum that standard grading does not make sense or grading is so misunderstood by the students that it causes problems. Pass/fail or satisfactory/unsatisfactory may be useful in these cases, with the criteria for each clearly expressed ahead of time to the students.

Another strategy that is effective with some students is to hold student-and-teacher conferences about progress made on specific goals the students are working on and then jointly rate progress toward these goals together. Videotapes of the students can be viewed jointly to discuss and rate social progress. A look at classwork can help the students review their progress.

Homework: Concept Development.

For some students with autism, alternatives to homework are the most efficient use of their time. One highly effective alternative to homework is to use the time at home on concept development. In this strategy parents work with the students to develop concepts and vocabulary that will be talked about in the next week in class. They may talk about, draw about, or find other material or pictures about upcoming topics through books, magazines, video, TV, or other means.

If assignments still require a certain amount of time spent outside the regular class schedule in the form of homework, this may be done most effectively with school staff in an alternative setting such as a resource room or school library. Greater assistance for students to complete the work or to be free from distractions can be achieved in these settings.

Essay Work: Outline Development.

Creative and original thinking can be very difficult for students with autism. Most students prefer factual or real-life types of projects. Students may experience great anxiety and tension over creative activities while finding a nonfiction paper interesting and enjoyable to write. For nonfiction projects some adults with autism have described a process in which detailed pictures or stories are first visualized as entire pieces in their heads before they put any of it on paper (Grandin, 1988).

Students with autism can do "creative" projects if they are given assistance to develop a plan first. When assigning a creative project, plan with the students to develop the outline and directions. Make the beginning and ending clear as to when it is finished and what it will look like.

Creative information or original ideas can often be obtained from students with the use of open-ended statements. An example of an open-ended statement to start planning a project is as follows: "When I want to write about _____ (or come up with a general topic for them), I think about _____." An outline for their work can be built from this using more open-ended statements, such as, "Tell me three things about (topic)."

When using the approach of asking for a specific number of responses from students using a visual grid is very effective. The visual grid shows the open-ended statement along with a blank (see Figure 3.5). The grid is a verbal worksheet in which the students fill in the answers by telling the teacher or parent their idea and the teacher or parent writes in the answer. It seems to disturb the flow of information when the students must write in the answer. Some students may get very involved in the process and ask to do some of the writing. This works effectively if it is the student's idea and the flow of thoughts is not interrupted too much.

Class Discussions: Advance Organizers.

Participation in regular class lessons or new

Vacations

3 things I like about vacations are:

1. _____

2. _____

3. _____

3 things I think are interesting about vacations:

1. _____

2. _____

3. _____

FIGURE 3.5. Example of a visual grid.

activities can be enhanced by some advance awareness of the material by the student with autism. To supply needed information Advance Organizers are used so that a teacher may prepare a student for new material. Some strategies in Advance Organizers are to introduce new concepts, teach new vocabulary, give an organizational framework for upcoming material, or give the student concrete objectives. Advance Organizers are usually visual to help the student anticipate and prepare. This may be as simple as studying a city map and bus schedule before actually making the trip. It can be as complex as visiting the library and researching material on new vocabulary before this is discussed in the classroom (Horton & Lovitt, 1989).

Stress: Asking For Help. The skills needed to ask for assistance from others involve a series of complicated decisions and levels of self-awareness. For many students with autism, this always remains a problem in at least some of the situations they encounter. To provide intervention in this area the teacher or parent can build in steps and strategies for seeking assistance or to have work checked. One method is to use cue cards as reminders to students to ask for help if they need it (see Figure 3.6). These

---

Ask Ms. Smith for help when you need it.

FIGURE 3.6. Help cue card.

cards can be taped in their notebooks or other prominent places where they will notice them.

Another strategy to remind students to ask for help is the use of visual signals. Check marks on work at various points to remind students to seek out the teacher to have their work checked is one signal that works well (see Figure 3.7).

A final strategy that is useful if the student is using a set of written directions is to add a direction such as, "Go to the teacher if you need help."

CHAPTER SUMMARY

In this chapter the characteristics of autism have been defined with an emphasis on how this disability affects learning style. Effective assessment of students with autism is tied to their characteristics and learning styles. After defining autism and assessing its impact on the educational process, a teacher or parent can develop a plan of support based on the two levels of assistance available—modifications and adaptations or interventions and direct assistance. It is important to avoid a recipe-book approach to providing support to students with autism. Understanding the impact of autism on individual students will help you decide the levels and types of supports needed and allow for maximum individualization.

Increased independence will be the outcome for the students.

Through increased independence it is possible for students with autism to find meaningful involvement in school. Teachers and parents have many strategies to employ; the greatest challenge is to match them to the needs of the students. Maximum independence and satisfying social relationships are possible.

REFERENCES

Cautela, J., & Groden, J. (1978). *Relaxation: A comprehensive manual for adults, children and children with special needs.* Champaign, IL: Research Press.

Dalrymple, N. (1987). *Home life checklist: Adolescents and young adults,* Bloomington, IN: Indiana Center on Autism.

Frith, U. (1989). *Autism: Explaining the enigma.* Cambridge, MA: Blackwell.

Frith, U. (1991). Asperger and his syndrome. *Autism and Asperger Syndrome.* New York: Cambridge University Press.

Grandin, T. (1988). Teaching tips from a recovered autistic. *Focus on Autistic Behavior, 3*(1), 1–8.

Grandin, T. (1990). Needs of high functioning teenagers and adults with autism (Tips from a recovered autistic). *Focus on Autistic Behavior, 5*(1), 1–16.

$$
\begin{array}{cccc}
38 & 46 & 84 & 56 \\
-12 & -11 & -39 & -44\checkmark \\
\\
23 & 14 & 99 & 17 \\
-11 & -3 & -81 & -5 \\
\\
52 & 43 & 21 & 7 \\
-16\checkmark & -31 & -10 & -2 \\
\end{array}
$$

Stop

FIGURE 3.7. When students see check marks, it is a signal to get the teacher to check their work.

Horton, S., & Lovitt, T. (1989). Construction and implementation of graphic organizers for academically handicapped and regular secondary students. *Academic Therapy, 24*(5), 625–640.

Janzen, J. E. (1986). Learning characteristics associated with autism, paper from the Oregon Department of Education, Statewide Regional Services for Autism, Salem, Oregon.

Janzen, J. E. (1989). Scheduling and schedules: A system to improve motivation and behavior, paper from the Oregon Department of Education, Statewide Regional Services for Autism, Salem, Oregon.

Janzen, J. E. (1992a). Serving students with autism: Predicting and reducing the intensity and frequency of behavioral crisis, paper from the Oregon Department of Education, Statewide Regional Services for Autism, Salem, Oregon.

Janzen, J. E (1992b). Understanding autism in the young child: Practical intervention strategies, paper from the Oregon Department of Education, Statewide Regional Services for Autism, Salem, Oregon.

Mesibov, G., & Troxler, M. (1988). Assessment in the classroom. In E. Schopler & G. Mesibov (Eds.), *Diagnosis and assessment in autism* (pp. 261–270). New York: Plenum.

Mesibov, G. B. (1990–91, Winter). Learning styles of students with autism. *The Advocate: Newsletter of the Autism Society of America, Inc.,* pp. 12–13.

Moreno, S. J. (1991). *High-functioning individuals with autism: Advice and information for parents and others who care.* Crown Point, IN: MAAP Services.

Murphy, D. A., Meyers, C., Olesen, S., McKean, K., & Custer, S. (1988). *Exception: A handbook for teachers of mainstreamed students.* Cushing, OK: CSDC.

Pefiesson, R. S., & Desser, P. R. (1989). *Semantic organizers.* Rockville, MD: Aspen.

Sacks, O. (1993/1994). An anthropologist on mars. *The New Yorker,* December 27, January 3.

Organization and Time Management Strategies

Phyllis Coyne

ORGANIZATION AND SEQUENCING DIFFICULTIES ASSOCIATED WITH AUTISM

Most young people have significant difficulties with organization, regardless of their intelligence or age. The purpose of this chapter is (1) to provide insight into the particular organizational challenges of autism and (2) to provide practical strategies to assist the young person with autism in organizing and developing their own self-management systems.

Organization may be complicated for all of us, but it is particularly challenging for young people with autism. Organization requires an understanding of what needs to be done and a plan for implementation. The interrelated and abstract nature of these requirements presents major barriers for young people with autism. They often become immobilized or unable to begin a task when there are organizational demands (Mesibov, 1990–91). Their difficulties with organization often interfere with their ability to use their other capabilities to complete a task. This is often mistakenly interpreted by people unfamiliar with autism as noncompliance or other behavior problems.

Jeremy provides an example of how this might appear. Jeremy is a 17-year-old student with autism who sat drawing a dot in the middle of the paper and talked to himself when he was instructed to create a word and picture map of what he was doing in his life now and what he wanted to do in five years. The instruc-

tor gave clear, step-by-step instructions and provided samples of completed maps, but Jeremy continued making the dot and talking to himself. He was able to start and complete the map only after the instructor made four dots on the page. This provided a structure so that he could start the map by drawing a rectangular box. Although writing and drawing a map of one's life is cognitively a difficult task for anyone, Jeremy's completion of his map indicated that he had the capacity to do the map. His problems were in organizing it and getting started.

Most young people with autism have difficulty doing organizational tasks without specific training. For instance, some bright students with autism may not be able to remember to bring their notebooks to class. Frequently these young people are carried organizationally by their parents and teachers throughout their school years. They are often unaware that others are taking care of an important aspect of life for them by providing organizational structure and time management. They may not know the importance of organization and may falsely believe that they are as ready for independent adult living as anyone else.

Figure 4.1 shows a young man with outstanding academic achievement in high school. He and his family have aspirations for him to attend an Ivy League School. However, he is dependent on his mother's organization of his assignments and materials to complete school work. His father has to remind him what and

FIGURE 4.1. Many persons with autism are dependent on others for organization.

when things need to be done. Without this assistance, this young man would not be able to maintain a schedule, let alone be successful in school. Unfortunately, the focus on academics is not enough to prepare him to meet his and his family's goal of attending Harvard. To be successful in any college setting, he must be able to organize and manage his life more independently.

This chapter introduces strategies for increased self-management of time, tasks, and materials in life. However, it is important for the reader to first understand the underlying reasons for these difficulties. The cognitive characteristics of autism in the areas of information processing, understanding time, sequencing, and compulsiveness significantly impact the organization and time management of persons with autism.

Information Processing

Organization is very conceptual. One must be able to see the whole picture and break it down into its component parts to organize. The manner in which young people with autism process information significantly affects their ability to organize. Although people without autism generally recognize the importance and benefits of being personally organized, many young people with autism lack an understanding of the value and importance of organization.

Organization requires an assignment of importance or priorities to activities. Young persons with autism have difficulty both knowing what to focus on and sorting out what is relevant (Frith, 1989). They may believe that any written information on paper, such as a handout, an assignment, a completed report, a note to parents, the lunch menu, or a school newspaper, has equal importance and put it all down in a haphazard manner. This often results in their having the messiest desks or lockers in the school. It sometimes, also, results in completed reports not being turned in to the teacher or notes not going home to parents.

Young people with autism often fail to realize that information or materials can be rearranged to produce an organized structure. If they are asked to put their papers in a notebook, they might insert them "as is" from their disorganized pile or only put in the papers that are of specific interest to them. They may collect every document related to an area of interest but have no basis for choosing what is important or ordering them.

These organizational difficulties lead to problems beyond high school. They can significantly affect job performance and household tasks. Chapter 1 cites Carpenter's statement that her organizational difficulty led to the loss of a job where she was well liked.

Understanding Time

Difficulty in understanding time also causes organization to be difficult for these young people. One young person with autism summed this up by saying, "I don't know what time is, but I know it's important." Even basic concepts such as "a minute," "later," and "wait" are abstract and difficult for them to understand. This problem understanding time concepts negatively impacts their ability to do temporal sequencing. They have difficulty with time management because it requires an analysis to predict, prepare, or anticipate the duration of an activity.

Sequencing

Difficulty in sequencing is another obstacle to organization for young people with autism. Sometimes they do not understand the importance of sequences. They have difficulty perceiving organization in a set of materials such as notes, texts, and assignments. This results in not only trouble dealing with multiple-step tasks such as assignments in an organized fashion, but also trouble dealing even with an isolated task in an organized fashion. Their concrete focus on specific details and poor ability to see relationships between them often causes difficulty remembering the precise order of tasks that have been outlined. Their distractibility adds to their difficulty keeping the order of events together in the proper sequence (Grandin, 1992).

A student with autism may complete homework and then not turn it in, because it is not perceived as part of the sequence. Another student may sit tapping her pencil, because she does not know where to start writing on a math paper. This same student may only need a red x in the upper-left-hand corner to start and complete the paper.

Routines and Rituals

Some young people with autism may compensate for their disorganization by developing rigid routines and rituals to make life more ordered. Sometimes they become obsessive or compulsive with self-management and appear to be superorganized. This may result in their having the neatest desks or lockers in the school. These young people often insist on sameness and become very upset if someone disturbs the order they have created (Moreno, 1991).

Unfortunately, these organizational attempts are seldom functional. For instance, one student always had to complete the paper he was working on before going to the next activity. This was a problem in classes that had assignments that took several classes to complete. Before beginning a task, another student had to sharpen all his pencils regardless of their sharpness. This was a problem when there was no pencil sharpener in the room or when his pencils were already short.

STRATEGIES TO HELP YOUNG PEOPLE WITH AUTISM ORGANIZE AND SELF-MANAGE

Many times the young person with autism relies on others to organize information and the environment. To function more effectively and independently, these young people need to be taught concrete ways to organize their own tasks, time, and materials. This section describes several strategies to improve organizational and time management skills of young people with autism. To be able to more independently manage time, tasks, and materials, young persons with autism need to

- understand the meaning and importance of organization,

- have an awareness of what organizational components are necessary for them, and

- have an individualized organization system that they can help create and self-manage.

Understanding the Purpose and Meaning of Organization

Young people with autism need a concrete explanation of the purpose and meaning of organization. This should include an explanation of how and why people organize their time and tasks in life. Since young people with autism often miss information that appears to be common knowledge, it is important to consider details that they may have missed. Using the word "sometimes" or providing multiple examples of a concept will help to avoid rigid thinking and misinterpretation.

Two concrete methods to present this type of information are (1) through the semantic organizer approach introduced in Chapter 3 and (2) through the social story format presented in detail in Chapter 5.

Figure 4.2 is an example of a semantic organizer about organization for a student who is not organizing to get her assignments done. This format is also sometimes referred to as clustering, webbing, or mapping. It is effective because it organizes and presents information in a visual/spatial mode that highlights relationships, sequences, and outcomes (Pefiesson & Denner, 1989). It additionally provides a permanent frame of reference. These organizers need to be individualized for the individual's

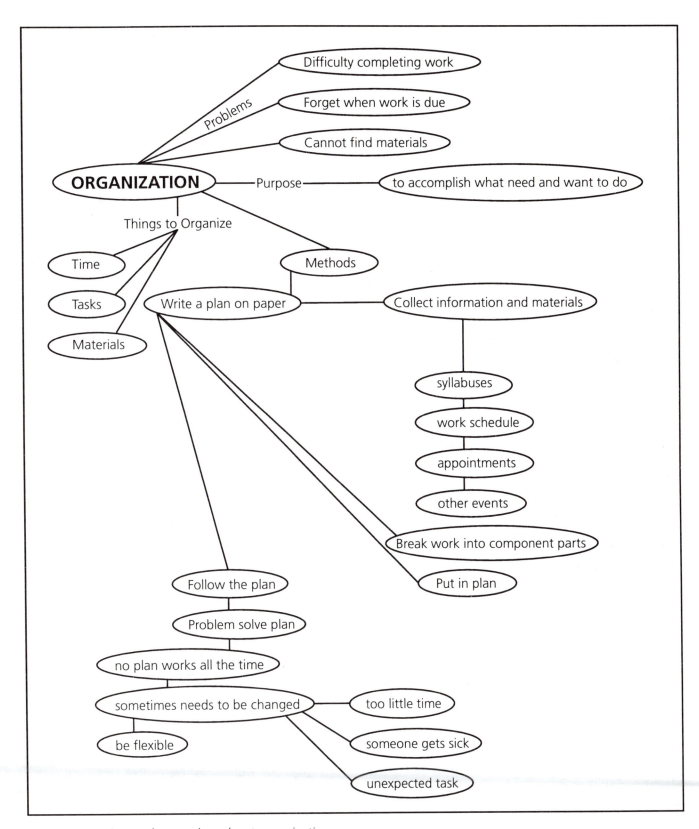

FIGURE 4.2. Semantic organizer about organization.

schemata or background knowledge and, whenever possible, created along with the young person with autism.

Awareness of Own Organizational Needs

Young people with autism are very compliant and will try to follow an organization system once it is taught to them. However, to begin to make decisions about how to organize and self-manage, all young people need an awareness of themselves and what is necessary or useful for them to accomplish a task. For instance, organization to learn and study at school and at home requires an awareness of factors that will enhance studying (Fry, 1991). Because many young people with autism lack insight regarding how they function and what their environmental and organizational needs are, they need careful assistance to gain awareness.

Figure 4.3 offers a sample format to help the young person with autism consider components of an ideal learning environment. Since answering open-ended questions is often difficult for the young person with autism, it utilizes a forced-choice approach.

Many young people with autism need help and further information to answer the types of questions listed in Figure 4.3. Both the characteristics of autism and the uniqueness of the individual need to be considered in providing guidance for self-awareness. Following are some key points to consider when providing assistance in answering these questions.

Type of Information. Generally, individuals with autism learn best from visual information. As they become more aware, some higher functioning individuals with autism express that they become overwhelmed and shut down when they get too much auditory information and not enough visual information. Since many individuals also have visual/spatial strengths, having hands-on experience may enhance learning.

Lecture Activity. Young people with autism generally do best when supported with visual infor-

mation. Since organizing note taking may be difficult, a note-taking guide or structured outline of the topic may be necessary. Sometimes teachers provide this structure; however, young persons with autism will be more independent if they recognize the need for this structure and are able to request it.

Classroom Placement. Consideration needs to be given to visual and auditory sensitivities, distractions, and optimum proximity of instructors, peers, or materials. Often young people with autism do best sitting in front and to the side, away from windows and doors. This offers minimum distraction and maximum closeness to a relevant source of information, the teacher.

Study Location. Young people with autism benefit from having a designated place to do assignments. In general, this should be in as quiet a location as is possible.

Study Time. It is important to set a regular time for studying and organizing. Young people with autism tend to have times of day when they are most alert and productive. Effectiveness often decreases in late afternoon and early evening.

Study Helpers. Although most young people with autism study best alone, it is also important for them to recognize sources of assistance while studying.

Sensory Input. Most young people with autism benefit the most from being in a quiet room. However, sometimes listening to acoustic music through headphones is helpful to block out auditory distractions and increase concentration.

Work Space. Young people with autism need a designated area for materials.

Breaks. Realistic scheduling of activities requires breaks. Young persons with autism need to know how long they can study before taking a break. This will be different for preferred and nonpreferred activities, as well as easy and

My Ideal Learning Environment

How I receive information best:

_____ Orally   _____ Visually   _____Manually

In the classroom, I should:

_____ Concentrate on taking notes   _____ Concentrate on listening

_____ Ask for structured outline of topic

_____ Sit in front   _____ Sit in back   _____ Sit near window or door

Where I study best:

_____ At home   _____ In the library   _____ In study hall

_____ Somewhere else: _____

_____ At desk   _____ At table   _____ At study carrel

Other: _____

When I study best:

_____ In the morning   _____ In the evening   _____ In the afternoon

_____ Before dinner   _____ After dinner

How I study best:

_____ Alone   _____ With a friend   _____ With parent or teacher help

_____ With music   _____ In front of TV   _____ In a quiet room

How I find work materials best:

_____ In desk   _____ In box by desk   _____ On bookshelf

Other: _____

When I need to take a break:

_____ Every 30 minutes or so   _____ Every hour   _____ Every 2 hours

_____ Every _____ hours

FIGURE 4.3. Format for learning environment form.

hard activities. For instance, a person may be able to do a difficult task for less than half an hour, but be able to do an easy task for two hours.

Individualized Organization System

Organizational demands increase for everyone in adolescence and adulthood. The young person with autism needs an individualized organization system to visually represent tasks that need to be accomplished and the time frame in which they need to be accomplished. Visual aids provide ongoing organization and structure as well as a built-in way for teachers, parents, and the young person with autism to recognize when a particular sequence of assignments has been accomplished. Three basic components are necessary for the organization system:

- individualized visual organizers for management of tasks,

- a visually coded work area for organization of materials and completion of tasks, and

- other visual supports to complete tasks.

Individualized Visual Organizers. Individualized visual organizers are valuable tools in time management for young persons with autism. Several methods that can be used with young persons with autism to create time management plans are (1) assignment folders, (2) planning charts, (3) time management calendar systems, and (4) monthly planning calendars.

Assignment Folders. An assignment folder offers an example of a system that keeps necessary papers and instructions in one place and can be incorporated into the type of looseleaf notebook used by many high school students (Figure 4.4). It can be made out of a standard two-pocket folder or two-pocket portfolio. The front pocket is labeled "To Be Completed" and holds papers to be completed. The back pocket is labeled "Completed Work" and holds completed assignments until they are turned in. An

assignment sheet is in the middle of the folder (Shields & Heron, 1989).

Many high school programs utilize assignment sheets for young people to track assignments. In addition, many of the commercially available student day planners and academic planners include assignment sheets. Although it is important for young people with autism to look as much like other students as possible, sometimes the existing system does not provide enough specific information or organization for them. They need the following information on each assignment: when due, what to do, materials needed, where to do it, and where to turn it in. In many cases the existing forms can be adapted for these young people (Figure 4.5).

Upon receiving an assignment the young person with autism fills in the next available line on the assignment sheet, listing the specifics of the assignment, materials needed, due date, place to do it, and where to turn it in. The assignment sheet can also serve as a guide to the information that the young person needs to get before beginning the assignment and a prompt to request missing information.

Initially, a teacher or assigned peer needs to monitor and offer assistance to ensure that all assignments are listed accurately, all papers are in the "To Be Completed" pocket, and all materials for completion are marked. Each night at a designated time, peers could make phone calls to their chosen "buddies" to ensure that their assignment sheets are accurate and that the assignments have been completed.

This system may need to be further individualized by using a color-coding system. For instance, a young person who forgets to gather materials may need to have the materials list highlighted in yellow. "Sticky notes" can be used to mark materials that are needed to complete the assignment.

Planning Charts. Young people with autism have trouble dealing with tasks that must be completed over time in an organized manner. Planning charts can provide the overall scope and sequence for projects that require completion over a long period of time and serve as a

FIGURE 4.4. Assignment folder.

Subject: _Math_   **Due Date**: _3/28_

Assignment: _Chapter 4 & 5_   **Materials Needed**: _Math Book_

_____   _Worksheet_

_____   _Pencil_

                                                        Eraser

Type: _____ Paper   _____ Project   _____ Test/Quiz Prep

    __X__ Worksheet   _____ Other

Work Location: __X__ Study hall   _____ Library   _____ Class

                            _____ Home   _____ Other

Place to Put Completed Assignment: _Folder on Mrs. Ali's desk_ _____

Subject: _Civics_   **Due Date**: _4/1_

Assignment: _Test Chapter 6 - 8_   **Materials Needed**: _Civics Book_

_____   _Notes_

_____   _Highlighter_

Type: _____ Paper   _____ Project   __X__ Test/Quiz Prep

    _____ Worksheet   _____ Other

Work Location: _____ Study hall   _____ Library   _____ Class

                            __X__ Home   _____ Other

Place to Put Completed Assignment: _Wire basket on Mr. Smith's desk_ _____

Subject: _Biology_   **Due Date**: _4/5_

Assignment: _Lab Journal_   **Materials Needed**: _Journal_

_____   _Pencil_

_____   _Calculator_

                                                        Worksheets

Type: __X__ Paper   _____ Project   _____ Test/Quiz Prep

    __X__ Worksheet   _____ Other

Place to Put Completed Assignment: _Box by door_ _____

FIGURE 4.5. Sample assignment sheet.

practical means for the young person with autism to determine the amount of time needed for each task. Tasks are broken down into smaller, more manageable segments, and the expected amount of time to complete each seg-

ment is written down, The chart can be left on the wall at home and completed steps in the process can be checked off as a self-monitoring system. Ready-made planning charts or calendars can be purchased from art supply, stationery, office supply, or book stores. An example of a usable format is shown in Figure 4.6.

The planning chart needs to be individualized for the types and amounts of information needed by the young persons with autism. In some cases, they may need more detailed information than in the sample planning chart.

Since young people with autism have problems identifying and sequencing parts, they need a structure and guidance to help them with the process of developing and using a planning chart. The semantic organizer approach presented in this chapter and the social story format described in Chapter 5 offer effective strategies for explaining how to break tasks into their component parts. A fill-in-the-blank guide or a checklist for the process can also be useful. Pairing the young person with a peer who is good at listing the steps in an assignment and at estimating how long each should take can be helpful in conjunction with one or more of the strategies above.

Time Management Calendar Systems. As our lives become more complex, most of us use a written schedule to organize ourselves and to accomplish tasks. Well-designed schedules can organize information regarding what to do, when to do it, how much to do, how long to do it, and what will happen next. Organized people make lists and tailor a personal organizer to fit their unique situations. The need for such time management and organization usually increases during the high school and adult years.

A variety of useful time management calendar systems are commercially available to combine school, work, and personal commitments in one place. The Trapper Keeper Binder and other binder organizers provide systems to keep schedules, assignments, notes, papers, and personal information together in one place.

Most of the commercially available personal organizers or time management calendar systems advocate the following steps:

	Month/Week	Project: Civics Paper	Review/Exam Schedule
Month 1	Week 1	Finalize topic (1 hr.)	Review civics notes (3 hr.)
	Week 2	Initial library research (2 hr.) General outline (1 hr.)	
	Week 3	Detailed library research (3 hr.) Detailed outline (1 hr.)	Review biology notes (4 hr.)
	Week 4	First draft (4 hr.)	Review math notes (4 hr.)
Month 2	Week 1	Second draft, spellcheck, proof (6 hr.) Independent proof (1 hr.)	Review civics notes (3 hr.)
	Week 2	Type final draft, proof (3 hr.)	Review biology notes (4 hr.)
	Week 3	Turn in project	Review math notes (4 hr.)

FIGURE 4.6. Sample planning chart.

- Write in school schedule, work schedule, appointments, and events.

- Create a "To Do List" of what you want to accomplish during the week.

- Prioritize in order of importance.

- Plan each day by moving items to be done to available spaces in the daily boxes.

Key guidelines in assigning time blocks for tasks are:

- Allow enough time.

- Devote most productive study times to most difficult tasks.

- Schedule study time in reasonable blocks of time with short leisure breaks in between.

Although these commercially available personal organizers or time management calendar systems can be used with young people with autism, they need to be adapted for individual needs. In some cases, additional steps or categories may be necessary. Visual coding can be used to call attention to specific categories. For instance, appointment times can be underlined so that they stand out. A highlighter can be used to make important items stand out. Color coding can further help organize. "Red" assignments might signal tasks that have an immediate deadline, whereas "green" assignments might not be due for a week. Different colors can indicate various items—e.g., red = work, blue = personal tasks, green = appointments, and orange = tasks.

Prioritizing tasks is one area in which young persons with autism are likely to need guidance. They have difficulty identifying what is relevant or most important. They might assign more importance to brushing the dog than studying for a final exam. They also may feel compelled to fit everything on their "To Do List" on their weekly calendar. They need to be taught that everything listed does not need to be accomplished that week. They also need a means to prioritize tasks in order of importance to ensure that assignments of the most importance get done. One question to ask is, "If I want to pass all my courses, what do I need to get done this week?"

A code system can be added to the "To Do List" to prioritize tasks. High priority or "must do" tasks can be marked with an H for high, tasks that are not urgent or can wait until next week can be marked with an L for low, and all other items can be marked with an M for medium. Tasks can be transferred to the daily or weekly schedule beginning with the ones identified as H. Nonurgent L tasks sometimes clutter up the schedule and can be put on a separate note page.

Figure 4.7 is one example of a time management calendar system. This weekly calendar shows school tasks to be completed as well as jobs to be performed inside or outside the home. "Materials" and "Comments" sections allow students to note any special assistance that might be needed. To allow persons with autism to manage their calendars more independently, watches are available that can be set to remind them of appointments via a little print-out display (e.g., "cookies for party").

Initially, young persons with autism are apt to need parents and teachers to help them plan the calendar and to support following the plan. The more that these young people are physically and cognitively involved in making some choices for their system, such as colors or symbols to organize the components, the more likely they are to understand and use the system. For any organization system to work, it has to be used and updated frequently. These young people will probably need some type of check-up system and varying degrees of ongoing support for the continued use of the personal organizer. It is important to establish a time with the young person with autism to sit down and plan for the following week. For instance, planning time on Sunday night could become part of the routine and be part of the weekly schedule. In adult life, some may need a personal manager to oversee issues and assist with planning.

Monthly Planning Calendars. Young people with autism may become anxious if there is no place to record something that needs to be done.

Things To Do This Week

School

	Task	Due	Time to Do
H	Math Chapter 4 & 5	3/28	3 hr.
H	Civics Test	4/1	3 hr.
H	Civics Paper - draft	4/21	4 hr.
H	Buy Lunch Tickets	3/25	15 min.

Home

Task	Due	Time
Wash Car	Sat.	1 hr.
Organize Sched.	Sun.	1 hr.
Books to Library	3/30	1 hr.
Call Bob 223-1234	3/26	10 min.
Buy Sega Game	Sun.	1 hr.

Work

Task	Time
Bike Gallery	4 - 8
	M,W,F

Schedule

	25 Monday	26 Tuesday	27 Wednesday	28 Thursday	29 Friday	30 Sat	31 Sun
Comments		Ask Mrs. Ali to check completed work		Turn in math papers			
Schedule	6 - 7 Exercise 8 - 3 School (Schedule on separate sheet) 4 - 8 Work 8:30 - 10:00 Homework	4 - 8 Work	4 - 8 Work		4 - 8 Work	Hike with Bob Clean Car - 1 hr. Library - 1 hr.	Computer City - Sega Game 1 hr. Organize Schedule 1 hr. Review for Civics test 1.5 hr.
Tasks/Time	Math 45 min. (Study Hall) Civics paper 1.5 hr.	Math 45 min. (Study Hall) Civics paper 1.5 hr.	Math 45 min. (Study Hall) Civics paper 1.0 hr.	Math 45 min. (Study Hall)	Review for Civics test - home - 1.5 hr.		
Materials	Library notes Outline Computer		Math book Worksheet Pencil & eraser		Civics book Civics notes Highlighter		

SCHEDULE

Year & Month — March 1995

FIGURE 4.7. Sample time management calendar.

Long-term projects, appointments, and events can be recorded in a monthly calendar. All the necessary information and materials for making a quality plan need to be collected. These include syllabuses, final exam schedule, work schedule, weekly class schedule, work schedule, family celebrations, trips, and other personal commitments (e.g., doctor appointments, club meetings, and extracurricular activities). All the information, including the steps of projects from the planning chart and the approximate time each is expected to take, go on the monthly calendar. Color coding could highlight which steps on the calendar go with which projects. Other important projects are added, and the calendar is revised as needed.

Organization of Personal Space and Materials

Young persons with autism need to monitor personal behavior by making certain that materials are organized in a way that ensures that all assignments will be completed and turned in on time. The young person with the messiest desk at school obviously needs frequent help with organization. However, all young people with autism can benefit from:

- a designated work area,

- labeled areas for materials,

- a visually coded organization system that utilizes containers,

- checklists or reminder cards that are posted in the work area, and

- an established work routine.

Containers for the organization system may include notebooks, folders, boxes, a card system, envelopes, baggies, jars, and/or paper clips. Checklists can help with the maintainance of organization. For some individuals a simple reminder card, rather than a checklist posted in the work area, may be enough (Figure 4.8).

It is important to establish a work routine so that the young person does not need to stop in order to plan where to begin and how to proceed.

Paper Management

Young people with autism have difficulty handling the infinite variety of written information. Part of the difficulty comes from not discriminating beween valuable and valueless papers. For instance, some young people with autism save all the mail and think that they need to respond to everything, including solicitations. These young people can be taught that there are three things that can be done with a piece of paper:

- throw it away,

- act on it, or

- file it for future reference.

"Put your materials in their designated container."

FIGURE 4.8. Reminder card.

A system to sort papers can be useful. This could include:

- a wastebasket;
- two file folders—one marked, "Things To Do" and the other marked, "To File";
- a file drawer or stand-up desk organizer.

Some young people may prefer pretty baskets, boxes, or other containers instead of file folders. In general, folders are the most practical. Tasks in the "Things To Do" folder can be transferred to the monthly calendar or appropriate place on the personal organizer. Papers in the "To File" folder need to be filed. The following basic filing principles can be taught to the young person with autism and posted as a checklist:

- Examine each piece of paper.
- Establish its reason for being in a file.
- Make file with broad categories.
- Place each paper in the labeled file folder that matches its category.
- File every folder in strict alphabetical order by its heading.
- Avoid any subgrouping.

Other Supports

Young people with autism may need additional visual information to help them organize and complete tasks. Many need written or picture directions or sequence lists that highlight the series of events and proper order to follow. This includes what to do and when, where, and how to do it. Examples of this type of support are provided in Chapter 3. Some may need materials in a container with the task made intrinsically clear through visual directions, a template, or the finished product as a model. Others may need visual definers, such as a line to show where to begin or end a paper or a kitchen timer to signal the beginning or end of an activity.

Some may need reminder cards. For instance, a young person may need a picture of a pencil on the cover of a notebook to remember to bring it to class. Another young person may need a checklist to get materials for assignments to be completed at home (Figure 4.9).

To move successfully from math to art and then to history class, one high school student needed a written schedule in his notebook, a map of the school with the location of his classes highlighted, and an individual work folder with class assignments and directions for each class, as well as an individualized reminder sheet regarding when and how to get assistance. Figure 4.10 is an example of a direction sheet for him for one art class.

Self-Management

The young person with autism needs to monitor personal behavior by making certain that materials are organized in a way that ensures that all assignments will be completed and turned in on time. Initially, parents and staff may need to develop organizational aids for the young persons with autism and teach them to use them. In the beginning, weekly desk and locker checks are likely to be necessary. If the organization system is used across all classrooms, it is likely that organizational skills will develop more quickly as well as more efficiently. The changing of classrooms and teachers in high school provides opportunities for generalization. Although young people with autism who have been taught an individualized organization system generally need less assistance in organization and time management over time, many will continue to need some degree of support or a check-in system throughout adulthood.

From the onset, it is important to involve the individuals in making choices about the systems that they want. Since young persons with autism may have a limited view of how and what can be done, these choices need to be structured. One way is to provide a forced-choice written format as in Figure 4.11.

Check your assignment sheet.

Get materials for homework.

Ask for help if you cannot find materials.

FIGURE 4.9. Example of checklist.

Art Activity: SILK SCREEN PAINTING—ST. PATRICK DAY CARDS

Amount: 5 St. Patrick's Day cards

Needed Materials: 5 sheets of paper, screen with frame, roller, ink, drying rack.

Directions:

  1. Get materials from silk screen shelf.

   Choose color of paper.

   Choose different color of ink.

   Choose screen pattern with frame.

  2. Put materials on your work area.

  Paper   Ink & roller   Screen & frame   Rack

  3. Insert paper in frame after teacher demonstration.

  4. Roll roller in ink and then over screen from left to right.

  Roller   Screen with frame

  5. Remove paper from screen and put on drying rack.

  6. Repeat #3–5 until you have 5 cards.

  7. Wash roller, screen, and your hands.

  8. Put materials back on silk screen shelf.

  9. Get ready for next class. You can talk with friends now.

FIGURE 4.10. Direction sheet.

My Organization Plan

Materials or activity that need to be organized:

_____

Possible solutions: Some ways that I could organize these materials or activity:

Materials

Organize in notebook and label sections   ☐ yes   ☐ no

Organize in box and label   ☐ yes   ☐ no

Sort by topic and color code   ☐ yes   ☐ no

Sort by topic and file   ☐ yes   ☐ no

Other _____

Other _____

Activity

Write down steps   ☐ yes   ☐ no

Make list with steps and target dates   ☐ yes   ☐ no

Put dates on calendar when to do steps   ☐ yes   ☐ no

Make a chart to monitor progress   ☐ yes   ☐ no

Other _____

Other _____

Action Plan: The way I will organize these materials or this activity is:

Action Steps	_Target Date_
_____	_____
_____	_____
_____	_____

Resources: People I can ask to assist me in organizing these materials or this activity:

1. _____

2. _____

3. _____

4. _____

Maintaining Organization: I will keep these materials organized by:

_____

_____

FIGURE 4.11. Sample organization plan.

CHAPTER SUMMARY

Organization is particularly difficult for young people with autism because of their unusual ways of processing information, understanding time, sequencing, and developing rigid routines. As a result, young persons with autism often rely on others to organize information and their environment. To function more effectively and independently, these young people need to be taught concrete ways to organize their tasks, time, and materials. This includes both helping the student to understand the importance of organization and basic organizational concepts, as well as assistance in establishing a usable organization system that the student can self-manage.

This chapter introduced strategies to assist young people with autism in understanding the importance of organization in their lives, in becoming aware of their own organizational needs, and in using an individualized organization system for increased self-management of time, tasks, and materials in life. Visual aids are utilized throughout to provide ongoing organization and structure, as well as a built-in way for teachers, parents, and the young person with autism to recognize when a particular sequence of assignments has been accomplished. The three major components of the organization system include individualized visual organizers for management of tasks, a visually coded work area for organization of materials and completion of tasks, and other visual supports to complete tasks.

Several methods presented that can be used with the young person with autism to create a time management plan are (1) assignment folders, (2) planning charts, (3) time management calendar systems, and (4) monthly calendars. It is vital that the young persons with autism be actively involved in the selection and development of their organizational structure so that they will like it and understand it. The more that these young people are physically and cognitively involved in making some choices for their system, such as colors or symbols to organize the components, the more likely they are to understand and use the system.

Although the goal is for young people with autism to organize and manage their time as independently as possible, they will probably need some type of check-up system and varying degrees of ongoing support for the continued use of the personal organizers.

REFERENCES

Frith, U. (1989). *Autism: Explaining the enigma.* Oxford: Blackwell.

Fry, R. (1991). *How to study.* Hawthorne, NJ: Career Press.

Grandin, T. (1992). An inside view of autism. In E. Schopler & G. Mesibov (Eds.), *High-functioning individuals with autism.* New York: Plenum.

Mesibov, G. (1990–91, Winter). Learning styles of students with autism. *The Advocate: Newsletter of the Austism Society of America,* pp. 12–13.

Moreno, S. (1991). *High-functioning individuals with autism: Advice and information for parents and others who care.* Crown Point, IN: MAAP Services.

Pefiesson, R., & Denner, P. (1989). *Semantic organizers.* Rockville, MD: Aspen.

Shields, J., & Heron, T. (1989). Teaching organizational skills to students with learning disabilities. *Teaching Exceptional Children, 21*(2), 8–13.

Social Assistance

Carol Gray

Historically, people with autism have demonstrated behaviors that have eluded the understanding of their parents, professionals, and peers. The literature often refers to the *social impairment in autism*, implying that the difficulties of social interaction lie solely within the person with autism. For the purposes of this chapter, it is important to recognize that this social *impairment* is *shared*—experienced not only by people with autism, but also by those who interact with them. The responsibility to improve any interaction is also shared, with effective social exchanges relying on the desire of each party to interact, understand, and be creative. The approaches described in this chapter are based on shared responsibility between adolescents with autism and their parents, professionals, and peers for improved social understanding and more effective social interactions.

All successful social interactions are basically part of a process of consideration and accommodation. They require an understanding of the individual characteristics of each person involved. For example, interaction with infants requires consideration of their early level of ability, unlike interactions with adolescents or with elderly persons. Making exaggerated faces may make a big hit with an infant, but the same approach will likely "turn off" an adolescent. Accommodation is also part of every successful social interaction. For example, people make logical and immediate accommodations for stroke victims who cannot speak, individuals who cannot hear, people who are unable to see, and people with laryngitis, to include them in social interactions.

This basic principle of consideration and accommodation in social interaction is nothing new. Stephen Covey, author of *The Seven Habits of Highly Effective People* (Covey, 1989), studied the habits of successful people over the last 200 years. He found that highly effective people had seven habits in common. In his chapter describing the fifth habit, "Seek First to Understand, Then to Be Understood," he discussed how people tend to rush to a solution before understanding the perspectives of others. He wrote, "We have such a tendency to rush in, to fix things up with good advice. But we often fail to take the time to diagnose, to really, deeply understand the problem first" (p. 237).

Three social interventions are described in this chapter: Comic Strip Conversations (Gray, 1994), Social Review (Gray, 1992), and Social Stories (Gray & Garand, 1993).[1] Based on a recognition that the quick exchange of information involved in traditional means of interaction is difficult for people with autism to understand, each of these interventions incorporates the use of visual supports. These visual supports make communication and social information easier for people with autism to understand (Gray &

---

[1]Additional materials and information regarding these approaches are available. Contact Future Education, 424 Lamar Blvd. East, Suite 102, Arlington, Texas 76011. Phone: (817) 277-0727 or FAX: (817) 277-2270. Or contact the author/editor of these materials, Carol Gray, at Jenison High School, 2140 Bauer Road, Jenison, MI 49428. Phone: (616) 457-8955 or FAX: (616) 457-2070.

Garand, 1993; Odor & Watts, 1991; Twachtman, 1992; Quill, 1992). Comic Strip Conversations yield insight into the perspective of the adolescent with autism. Simple stick figures and social symbols serve to illustrate a conversation between the adolescent with autism and another person. These conversations explore problem situations and visually identify new solutions. Social Review uses review of videotaped situations to assist parents, professionals, and peers in understanding how an adolescent with autism perceives a situation and often results in the adolescents independently identifying new responses they could make in that situation. Social Stories share accurate social information and identify expected responses to a situation. These individualized short stories are written following a special format and guidelines that are based on the learning style of individuals with autism. Together, these three approaches socially assist adolescents with autism and those who work with them.

WHAT IS SOCIAL ASSISTANCE?

The three social interventions described in this chapter—Social Review, Comic Strip Conversations, and Social Stories—are based on the concept of *social assistance*. Social assistance is just that—assistance, not control. To effectively assist adolescents with autism, it is important to respect their individual strengths and abilities, working together toward improved social skills.

Specifically, social assistance has three components: (1) improving the understanding and consideration others have of the unique perspective of the person with autism; (2) providing accurate social information, including help in predicting, understanding, and reading social situations; and (3) help and support in discovering new, more effective responses to social situations. These three components of social assistance are described in detail in this section.

Understanding the Unique Perspective of the Person with Autism

Chapters 1 and 2 of this book have focused on understanding how people process social information and the unique social challenges faced by adolescents with autism. By the time a person reaches adolescence and adulthood, the complexity of the judgments required for effective social interactions increases. One way to conceptualize this is by imagining each person has a *social file cabinet.* Located in the brain, this file cabinet contains hundreds of individual file folders, labeled with the names of people at work, at home, and in the community. Each file contains a wealth of individual information regarding a person's beliefs, past experiences, strengths, weaknesses, and personality. In a social situation, people rely as much on their personal social file cabinets as they do on the manners and social skills they have learned from parents and teachers (see Figure 5.1).

Each file is "pulled" automatically as a reference for every social interaction throughout the day. For example, Steve is walking to work and sees his friend, Tom. Steve pulls Tom's "social file" automatically. The extensive file is quickly reviewed, and *relevant* information is selected (see Figure 5.2).

Using information from Tom's file and an interpretation of Tom's current behavior, Steve greets Tom. "Tom! How's it going? Hey, I see you are in a hurry. I'll call you tonight. I have some questions about the wedding!"

The wealth of social information Steve stores in his social file cabinet makes possible successful social judgments and interactions, ties current experience to past encounters, and automatically guides his social responses. For example, sharing a personal problem is saved for the next time Tom comes around, or maybe Tom receives a call that evening when everything has slowed down.

Throughout the day, social files serve as a personal and detailed reference. The girl at the drive-thru window is there every Tuesday and

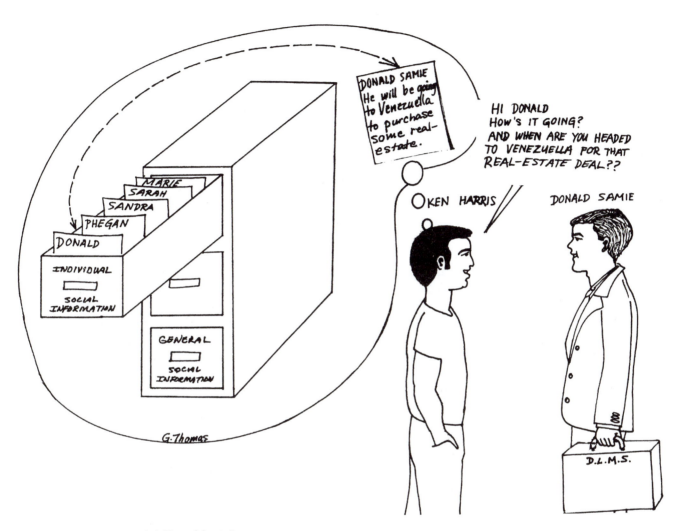

FIGURE 5.1. The "social file cabinet."

receives a nod of recognition. The boss is a stickler about cleanliness, and prior to her arrival at 9 a.m., the place is tidied. The boss is also not fond of small talk, is strict about proper use of break times, and likes people to check with her daily regarding the day's goals. As a result, the boss receives a greeting and is asked what needs to be accomplished during the day.

In addition to files about people, the social file cabinet contains general social information. These files contain information regarding the rules governing specific situations, general social cues, emotions, social expectations, and manners. While children are taught some of the information contained in these files, they have the ability to "mix and match" information from several files in response to the unique situations they encounter. Using Steve and Tom as an example, if the interaction happened to occur in a library, both parties would whisper, drawing on information from the "Tom" file and the "Social Behavior in the Library" file simultaneously.

For adolescents with autism, social information is often misinterpreted or difficult to understand. Social information may be "misfiled," making it difficult to retrieve and apply it effectively to new situations. Without common threads of social information that appear in many of the files, it is difficult to learn and generalize social skills and to know when to apply

> Tom is a hard worker and a trusted friend.
>
> Tom is getting married in one year.
>
> Last week Tom invited me to be his best man in his wedding.
>
> Whenever Tom and I talk politics, the conversation gets long and sometimes heated.
>
> Tom looks like he is in a hurry because he is fiddling with his watch.
>
> Whenever Tom is in a hurry it never fails—he fiddles with his watch.

FIGURE 5.2. Excerpts of relevant information from Steve's "Tom" file.

each rule. Often the skills that are taught to adolescents with autism do not "make sense," adding frustration to an endless number of situations that seem to defy understanding.

In addition, the social challenge experienced by individuals with autism is continually compounded by a second social impairment—the assumptions and misinterpretations others give to their responses and behavior. If teachers, parents, and friends do not understand how an individual with autism perceives a situation, they run the risk of responding to that person inappropriately. For example, an irritated substitute teacher indicates to an unruly class, "Everyone sit down." Interpreting the direction literally, Jenny, a student with autism, sits down immediately in the aisle between the desks. Reprimanded for "goofing off," Jenny is confused. *Following directions is goofing off?* The social rule of following directions that Jenny has struggled to learn—a skill she has applied in this class—suddenly does not apply.

The importance of improved mutual understanding between individuals with autism and others cannot be overemphasized. An accurate understanding of the motivation of an individual with autism results in more effective responses from parents, peers, and professionals. For example, using the example of Jenny and the substitute teacher, had the substitute understood Jenny's tendency to interpret communication literally, the substitute's response would have been different. The substitute may have simply redirected Jenny to sit in her seat. Not only would this correct

the situation, it would result in less confusion for Jenny. Efforts to understand the perspective of the individual with autism lead to a more accurate interpretation of what may initially be seen as a "problem behavior" or a "bad attitude." Increasing time spent understanding the problem from the perspective of the adolescent with autism decreases time spent searching for and implementing an effective solution.

Assistance in Predicting, Understanding, and Reading Social Situations

Assistance in prediction includes activities and materials that help a person with autism anticipate the social cues and implications of an upcoming social situation. For example, a school dance is scheduled for Friday. An individual with autism may need social information about school dances. Answers to *Who, What, When, Where,* and *How* questions provide information that helps an adolescent predict and plan for a situation. For example, information regarding the day, time, location, number of people, type of music, typical dress, how to ask someone to dance, how to get there, and so forth, may help the person with autism relax in anticipation of this new social activity and provide an opportunity to "rehearse" the situation in advance. The relaxation, in turn, improves the ability of the person with autism to respond effectively to the situation.

Assistance in understanding a social situation includes information provided in answers to *Why* questions. This is information most people take for granted and includes "automatic" social insights that govern social behavior. Understanding a social situation requires information about the thoughts, feelings, and motivations of others, the reasons for certain procedures, activities, and responses, social implications specific to a given situation, or descriptions of plans and activities behind the scenes. This is often the most critical, and at the same time the most difficult, information to share with adolescents with autism. "Why" information "seems too obvious" and is often omitted or overlooked. Assisting adolescents with autism in understanding social situations requires others to learn the art of observation and the ability to note and share the obvious.

Assistance in reading social situations includes efforts to help a person with autism identify the relevant cues in a social situation. Cues relevant to the school dance may include when to dance, when to ask someone to dance, or what it means when the deejay says, "Clear the floor" or "Couples only." In addition to identifying relevant cues, the possibility for variations or exceptions to those cues is also described. With this social information, a person with autism is better equipped to respond confidently, at the right times, to the variety of changes that occur in a given situation.

Assistance in Responding to Social Situations

Assistance in responding to social situations includes efforts to help the adolescents with autism identify their *own new responses* to a challenging situation or define possible solutions. For example, having reviewed written information about the dance, a person with autism may indicate that she "knows what to do now." This person may only need assistance identifying a few strategies to recall and use the information at the dance. A different person with autism may require more detailed information regarding what to do at the dance. Assistance in responding requires sensitivity to the support that persons with autism need,

recognizing and responding to their increasing confidence and independence.

All the approaches described in this chapter—Social Review, Comic Strip Conversations, and Social Stories—give functional application to the components of social assistance just described. Applying social assistance through these materials and activities provides opportunities for improved social interactions between individuals with autism and their teachers, friends, parents, and other professionals (see Figure 5.3).

COMIC STRIP CONVERSATIONS

Comic Strip Conversations are the working definition of the phrase, "the art of conversation." A Comic Strip Conversation is a conversation that incorporates the use of color and simple drawings to improve clarity of social interactions for persons with autism. Each person involved in the conversation draws while he or she talks to illustrate important concepts and ideas. These drawings structure an ongoing conversation, providing support to those who struggle to understand the quick exchange of information in a conversation.

Comic Strip Conversations are based on the belief that visualization (Grandin, 1992) and visual supports, found useful in structuring the learning of students with autism (Gray & Garand, 1993; Odor & Watts, 1991; Twachtman, 1992; Quill, 1991, 1992), may also improve their understanding and comprehension of conversation. In addition, the use of conversation symbols and color is intended to visually structure conversational skills, which are abstract and more difficult for students with autism to understand. Those familiar with mind mapping (Wycoff, 1991) will see similarities and may find it helpful to conceptualize the process of Comic Strip Conversations as similar to a map of a conversation.

While Comic Strip Conversations are very similar to any conversation in the sharing of ideas about the past, present, and future, other characteristics of Comic Strip Conversations are unique. These conversations follow a given

1. **Social assistance through improved understanding**

   - prevents responses by others to the adolescent with autism that are confusing from the perspective of the adolescent with autism, and that compound the social impairment.

   - results in logical and effective responses.

2. **Social assistance in predicting, understanding, and reading social situations includes**

   - assistance in anticipating an upcoming situation and its social implications.

   - assistance through information that answers "Wh" questions.

   - assistance in identifying social cues.

3. **Social assistance in responding to social situations includes**

   - assistance to the adolescent with autism in identifying solutions to social challenges or defining new responses.

FIGURE 5.3. The three components of social assistance.

structure to organize a social exchange and build in predictability. Comic Strip Conversations systematically identify what people say and do and emphasize what people *may be thinking.* Symbols, drawings, and written words simultaneously accompany the exchange of verbal information, with the joint attention of those involved focused on the drawing surface. This visual display assists parents, professionals, and peers in sharing information with individuals with autism. In addition, Comic Strip Conversations may provide insight into the perspective of the person with autism, assisting in the identification and expression of ideas that may be confusing.

Materials

As mentioned earlier, a Comic Strip Conversation is drawn by those involved in the interaction. This requires the use of drawing materials. A wide range of materials may be used for a Comic Strip Conversation. Minimally, pencils and paper are all that is required. Crayons, colored markers, or colored pencils may also be used. Chalkboards provide a large working area but have to be erased and cannot be referred to over extended periods of time. Laminate marker

boards and markers enable the use of a wide range of colors but again cannot be saved permanently.

The adolescent with autism is involved in the selection of conversation materials. Many factors determine which materials are selected. Some materials may be more interesting or easier to work with for an adolescent than others. Materials that allow participants to draw and write in a variety of colors may be critically important when discussing feelings. A conversation that discusses a problem situation and/or identifies new social skills may require the use of materials that can be saved for future reference (e.g., notebooks). Involving persons with autism in experimenting with and selecting materials for a given situation maintains their control of the support given to each conversation.

Procedure

Comic Strip Conversations are cumbersome if used with every interaction; they are intended to be used only during specific conversations. Important conversations warrant illustration. These may be conversations critical to an adolescent's transition from school to adult life, focusing on problem solving, future situations that are new or unfamiliar, or issues deemed important by any of the involved persons.

The person with autism initially takes the lead in a Comic Strip Conversation, with parents, professionals, or peers serving as guides to the conversation. The person with autism is assisted in selecting and expressing relevant ideas, though all parties to a conversation may draw or write at any time. A Comic Strip Conversation often sounds more like an interview in the beginning, with the person with autism responding to questions. Over time the goal is to work toward Comic Strip Conversations that sound less like interviews and more like conversations.

Simple, easy-to-draw symbols are a part of every Comic Strip Conversation. A special set of symbols, listed in the Conversation Symbols Dictionary, *look like* the abstract social concepts they represent (see Figure 5.4). Since individuals will each have certain topics they discuss often, they may want to develop their own symbols to represent ideas, objects, or situations that frequently occur in their conversations.

A Comic Strip Conversation begins with "small talk." While topics like the weather may not seem worth drawing about, beginning a conversation this way accomplishes two things. First, the conversation starts in a way similar to a typical conversation, illustrating the importance of beginning an interaction with small talk. Second, small talk provides the opportunity for everyone involved to "warm up" to drawing while talking before tackling tougher issues.

Often a situation that is giving an individual with autism difficulty is the topic of a Comic Strip Conversation. To begin the conversation, identify the setting by placing a location symbol in the upper-left-hand corner. For example, Susan has a new job at "Mr. Green's Kitchen," a local restaurant, and recently encountered a situation in which her boss's response was confusing. Susan discusses the situation with her case manager using a Comic Strip Conversation. Each Comic Strip Conversation begins by identifying where the situation takes place by placing a location symbol or written words in the upper-left-hand corner of the paper. Beginning her conversation

with her case manager, Susan writes, "Mr. Green's Kitchen" in the upper-left-hand corner of the paper.

The interaction is illustrated as it progresses, with the individual with autism speaking and drawing in response to questions and statements. Information covered in a Comic Strip Conversation includes who was there, what happened, what was said, and what people were thinking when they said certain things. Figure 5.5 lists a series of sample questions to guide Susan's drawings about the situation at work.

After covering where a situation occurs, who is there, and what is done and said, Comic Strip Conversations focus on what people in the situation may be thinking (see the information regarding social cognition in Chapter 1). While it may be easy for the individual with autism to identify what he or she is thinking, it is often more difficult to identify what others are thinking. Continuing with Susan's example, she identifies her own thoughts and feelings easily but experiences difficulty identifying Mr. Green's feelings about the same situation. Susan says she felt uncomfortable arriving late for work but expresses confusion regarding what Mr. Green was thinking about her late arrival. Mr. Green said, "Glad you finally made it here with the rest of us!" Susan interprets his response literally, believing that Mr. Green was feeling happy in response to her late arrival. This doesn't make sense to Susan, who wonders why Mr. Green likes it when she's late. The resulting drawing from Susan's Comic Strip Conversation visually describes the situation, expresses her confusion, and allows her case manager the opportunity to introduce other possible interpretations of Mr. Green's statements (see Figure 5.6).

Literal interpretations or misunderstandings are clarified using a Comic Strip Conversation. Color is incorporated to identify the motivation of each person involved in the situation being discussed (covered later). In addition, discussion with the individual with autism to explain the misunderstanding may be selective. To address Susan's literal interpretation of Mr. Green's response, color is incorporated to clarify the emotional content of what Mr. Green said and to assist Susan in understanding Mr. Green's perspective.

FIGURE 5.4. The Conversation Symbols Dictionary.

---

1. **Where are you?**

   (draw person)

2. **Who else is here?**

   (draw person)

3. **What are you doing?**

   (draw relevant items, actions)

4. **What happened? What did others do?**

   (draw relevant items, actions)

5. **What did you say?**

   (use talk symbol)

6. **What did others say?**

   (use talk symbol)

7. **What did you think when you said that?**

   (use thought symbol)

8. **What did others think when they said that/did that?**

   (use thought symbol)

FIGURE 5.5. Sample Comic Strip Conversation questions.

Before closing a Comic Strip Conversation, the topic of conversation is summarized. The drawings may appear to run into one another or look a little confusing, yet those involved in a conversation are often able to "read it back" almost verbatim using the drawings and symbols as an outline. As a conversation is reviewed by its participants, numbers may be placed to identify the sequence of events. Summarizing a conversation serves to organize the ideas and identifies relevant events prior to identifying possible new solutions to the situation.

A Comic Strip Conversation is concluded with the identification of new solutions. These may be written on a new paper. At first, as many solutions as possible are listed. The individual with autism uses a highlighter to identify the best solution. In some cases it may be helpful to identify the solutions in the order in which they will be implemented. For example, since Mr. Green is unhappy with Susan's late arrival at work, Susan decides to get up 15 minutes earlier each morning. She also decides on two additional backup solutions: apologizing in the event of a late arrival and offering to work additional time to compensate for time lost.

The use of color in a Comic Strip Conversation identifies the emotional content or motivation behind a statement, thought, or question. By assigning colors to written words to reflect their emotional content, individuals with autism are visually assisted in recognizing the importance of feelings and motivation in communication. The Color Chart lists colors that may be used to identify feelings and motivations. According to the Color Chart, Mr. Green's statement, "Glad you finally made it here *with the rest of us!*" is written in red to reflect the anger he felt when making the comment (see Figure 5.7).

FIGURE 5.6. Sample drawing from a Comic Strip Conversation.

FIGURE 5.7. Comic Strip Conversations Color Chart.

Summary of Comic Strip Conversations

A Comic Strip Conversation is a communication tool used with adolescents with autism to clarify important interactions with simple drawings. Comic Strip Conversations follow a structure that systematically covers who is involved in a situation, what they say and think, and what they do. This adds predictability to a conversation and structures the expression of ideas. These illustrated conversations incorporate the use of written words, simple drawings, and symbols. In addition, color is used to identify the feelings and motivations of others. Comic Strip Conversations often provide insight into the perspective of individuals with autism regarding a specific situation or social skill, insights that may be valuable in finding logical solutions to problems or in writing a social story.

SOCIAL REVIEW

Social Review informally assesses the perspective of the adolescent with autism, shares accurate information, and provides opportunity to identify new responses to the situation. Through the review of selected video clips, ideas are recorded in writing to clarify communication and to keep information available for future reference.

First, the adolescent responds in writing to specific questions about the videotaped event. This is followed by the parent, peer, or professional responding to the same questions in writing. Both perspectives are regarded as valid and are compared. Finally, Social Review provides an adolescent with autism the opportunity to determine his or her own new, more effective responses to the problem. This section begins with a description of the basic steps in Social Review, followed by a case example illustrating the use of Social Review with Mark, a secondary student with autism.

Basic Steps to Implementing Social Review

Social Review begins with the identification of a target situation, skill, or behavior that is causing the adolescent with autism difficulty. The problem is identified in writing with the adolescent with autism. The Social Review activity is described to the adolescent with autism. For conversations like this, where important information is shared with an adolescent with autism, a computer may be helpful. The information is typed into the computer, and the adolescent may take a copy of the interaction for future reference. With consent, the adolescent with autism is videotaped in the situation that is causing difficulty.

The next step in Social Review is preparation of all materials. Most importantly, this includes a short, representative video clip of a situation that is giving an individual with autism difficulty. Also needed are a video player and monitor, a large writing surface, markers, and a quiet, comfortable room.

A Social Review discussion is guided by a series of questions, similar to questions used in Comic Strip Conversations (see Figure 5.5). First, questions focus on the physical features of a situation—for example, location, furniture, equipment, or relevant objects. These are followed by questions concerning relevant people, what they say, and what they do. Finally, why the people behaved as they did is discussed.

The review of the videotape by the adolescent with autism is followed by a similar review completed by the parent, professional, or peer. This person restates the identical questions asked of the adolescent, writing the answers as he or she speaks. The perspective of a parent, peer, or professional is usually different from that of the adolescent with autism. Care is taken to matter-of-factly present information without discrediting the answers just recorded by the adolescent with autism.

A comparison of the adolescent's answers and those of the parent, peer, or professional is completed. Answers to questions regarding the physical setup of the situation (location, objects) are likely to be the same. The agreement in answers to questions is brought to the attention of the adolescent, as are those areas in which the answers are different. Answers that are in conflict are referred to as "opinions." This equalizes the validity of the perceptions of each person and supports the adolescent with autism as he or she learns about a new perspective. Comparing answers requires ample time for the adolescent with autism to consider new information and ask questions.

The final step in Social Review is the identification of new, more effective responses to the situation. As a result of the comparison of answers in the previous step, the adolescent may independently identify new solutions to the problem. An adolescent may need assistance from the parent, professional, or peer to identify solutions. Together with the adolescent, several solutions may be listed in a "brainstorm" approach, then reviewed and considered individually.

---

1. **Identify a target situation.**
   - Identify the target situation in writing with the adolescent with autism.
   - Inform the adolescent with autism of the basic steps of Social Review in writing.

2. **Prepare all materials.**
   - Prepare a representative video clip(s) of the target situation.
   - Also needed are a video player and monitor, a large writing surface, markers, and a comfortable room.

3. **Guide the observations of the adolescent with autism.**
   - Ask questions to guide the discussion, focusing first on location, followed by people, activities, statements, and motivators.
   - Responses of the adolescent with autism are written on the large tablet.

4. **A parent, professional, or peer responds to the same questions.**
   - Record answers in writing.

5. **Compare responses.**
   - Discuss areas where there is agreement.
   - Present areas of disagreement as "opinions."

6. **Identify new responses.**
   - Ensure opportunity for adolescent with autism to identify solutions independently based on the comparison of responses.
   - Peer, professional, or parent may identify new responses with the adolescent with autism.

7. **Monitor progress.**
   - Discuss progress with the adolescent with autism.
   - Possibly repeat the Social Review activity using current video clips showing improvement in the social skills of the adolescent with autism.

FIGURE 5.8. Steps for implementing Social Review.

The adolescent is monitored following a Social Review session. This will include discussions with the adolescent or others involved and perhaps direct observations or videotaping of the target situation. A second review of the videotape may be indicated, or a social story may be used to support the adolescent's improved social skills. Reviewing a videotape of the adolescent's improved behavior reinforces his or her success. Involving the adolescent and focusing attention on the benefits of newly acquired skills are central to continued success (see Figure 5.8).

A Social Review Case Example

Mark is a secondary student with autism attending a general education class in market-ing. Mark continually interrupts his marketing teacher, Mr. Richards. This is disruptive in Mark's class, where Mark comments in response to almost everything Mr. Richards says. Mark does not raise his hand or wait for a turn to speak. Mark's interrupting has persisted despite several discussions and positive behavioral interventions. The behavior continues despite Mark's repeated promises to stop interrupting.

Mark's difficulty with interrupting becomes dramatically apparent during a school assembly. Mark is concerned about the change in the schedule as a result of the assembly. The speaker opens his presentation by indicating that his topic is "Change." This immediately brings a loud verbal response from Mark, who begins talking to the speaker and interrupts the assembly.

FIGURE 5.9. Illustration of a Social Review activity.

A videotape of the speaker at the assembly is selected for Social Review by Mark's special education consultant, Mr. Adriansen. Two video clips are selected for Mark to review. The first clip lasts a few seconds and shows many students seated for an assembly with the speaker at the front of the room. The second clip is about one minute and shows Mark interrupting the assembly. Mr. Adriansen gathers all Social Review materials prior to meeting with Mark.

Mark is shown a short clip of the videotape and observes himself interrupting the speaker. During this review Mr. Adriansen periodically pauses the videotape, asking Mark to write answers to several questions. These questions provide Mark the opportunity to share his perspective of the situation (see Figure 5.9).

Mark's answers provide insight into his current problem with interrupting. Mark repeatedly identifies himself and the speaker as the *only people* at the assembly. Mr. Adriansen draws Mark's attention to the other students and teachers, and after several minutes Mark agrees that there are many people at the assembly. He writes this information down. Mark goes on to describe how the speaker is talking just to him and that the laughter of others is due to the fact that everyone feels the same as he does. He does not recognize that the laughter is in response to the fact that he interrupted the speaker.

Mark's description of the situation helps Mr. Adriansen understand Mark's perspective. The concept of *interrupting* holds little meaning for Mark. To appreciate the implications of interrupting, a person must first understand that others are listening to another person, in this case to the speaker at the assembly. Mark does not understand the social significance of other people at the assembly. Mark believes that the speaker is talking only to him, and he is answering him.

Using the example from the assembly, Mr. Adriansen writes his responses to the same questions asked of Mark. Mr. Adriansen and Mark compare the two written descriptions of the situation—Mark's and that of Mr. Adriansen. Mr. Adriansen refers to each description of the situation as an *opinion*, pointing to the writ-

ten answers while verbally summarizing each person's perspective.

Mark decides he can "stop interrupting." Mark lists in writing several things he needs to do to stop interrupting, including raising his hand when he wants to speak in class, waiting for a turn to speak, and listening while others are talking. He takes the list to Mr. Richards in marketing class and requests that his seat be moved next to the wall. Mark posts his list to the right of his desk. This list serves as a written reminder to Mark of his decision to stop interrupting and the skills he needs to demonstrate to accomplish his goal. Mark's interrupting in class ceases immediately.

What is important in Mark's case is his ability to identify a logical solution once he has accurate social information presented in a format he understands. Mark did not recognize or understand the social significance of other students in the classroom or at the assembly. Based on new, accurate social information presented in writing, Mark demonstrates that he has the ability to determine his own logical solution to his difficulty with interrupting.

Summary of Social Review

Social Review is an activity that reviews social situations that are causing difficulty; compares the perspective of the adolescent with autism with that of a parent, professional, or peer; and identifies more effective responses to the situation. The use of short video clips provides the adolescent with visual supports as a social situation is discussed. Questions regarding *who, what, when, where,* and *why* structure the activity, with both the adolescent with autism and the parent, professional, or peer writing their answers. Comparison of the two perspectives leads to the identification of new responses to the situation.

SOCIAL STORIES

A social story is a short story written in a special style and format that describes social situations in terms of relevant social cues and common responses. Social stories may be used to assist adolescents with autism with a variety of situations and skills, including understanding routines and variations in schedule, describing future events, defining a specific social skill, explaining the ever-changing and increasingly complex social interactions of young adults, expanding on social skills identified in social skill training programs, preparing for transition to adult life in the community, translating goals into understandable steps, explaining emotions and the thoughts and feelings of others, and any other relevant topic. With individualized social information in writing, young adults have control of a useful and accurate reference regarding the social situations that are difficult to understand.

Social stories are written by parents, professionals, or peers. By the time persons with autism reach adolescence, they assist in the writing and development of social stories. Social stories are most likely to be effective with persons with autism who have the ability to comprehend written material. The ability to read is not a necessity, as written material may be simplified with the use of symbols, simple illustrations, audiocassette tapes, or videotapes.

Basic Steps for Writing Social Stories

Topics for social stories are easily identified. Topics are determined by social skills or situations that are particularly challenging for an individual. Topics for social stories may be the result of insights gained through Social Review or Comic Strip Conversations. These activities often reveal misperceptions or misunderstandings that may be clarified with a social story. In addition, an individual's responses to questions about a specific social situation may indicate the need for a social story.

Social stories begin with careful observation and collection of information. Observing a situation prior to writing a social story ensures the necessary details to make the information relevant and accurate for the adolescent with autism. It is important to identify factors that

are not directly observed—for example, possible changes in routine, people, or expectations. Writing the possibility of variation into a story ensures its accuracy, an important feature for adolescents with autism who may interpret information literally.

Social stories are the result of two carefully written drafts, the rough draft and the final draft. The rough draft is written by a parent, professional, or peer. The final draft incorporates the feedback of many individuals, including the person with autism. Especially when writing for adolescents with autism, it takes more than one author to write a social story start to finish as a final draft.

Behind every social story is respect for the perspective of the adolescent with autism as valid. Efforts to determine how the adolescent perceives and interprets a given situation are critical. This perspective provides the focus of the social story. The focus of a social story determines which details should be included in a story. For example, if a person with autism is fearful of a given situation, the social story will have a different focus than if that same person were confused by the situation. Identifying the focus of a social story serves as a guide for where to begin and what to include.

Social stories are comprised of four basic types of sentences: *descriptive, directive, perspective,* and *control* sentences. Descriptive sentences objectively define where a situation occurs, who is involved, what they are doing, and why. Directive sentences are positive statements of desired responses. They often follow descriptive sentences, telling a student what is expected as a response to a given cue or situation. Directive sentences often begin with "I can," "I will," or "I will work on." Perspective sentences describe the reactions and feelings of others in a given situation.

A fourth type of sentence, the *control sentence,* is particularly applicable for use with adolescents with autism. Control sentences describe visual images that may help in recalling, understanding, and applying abstract information. Control sentences are written by the adolescent with autism after reading the rough draft of a social story. For example, a social story describes how people sometimes change their minds. The adolescent with autism may add the following control sentence to the story: "When someone says they 'changed their mind,' I can think of someone writing down words, erasing them, and writing down something new."

The most important sentences in social stories are descriptive, perspective, and control sentences. A good formula to follow to develop a social story is to write a total of four to six descriptive, perspective, and control sentences for every directive sentence in a story (see Figure 5.10). This ensures that the story includes important social information and guards against stories that are too directive and sound like a drill sergeant's checklist.

The most common mistake in writing social stories is the tendency to include too many directive sentences. This is particularly true when writing for adolescents, who may be insulted by directive sentences that seem logical and obvious in light of the information contained in the rest of the story. For this reason,

---

1. **Identify the topic.**
   - Topics are skills or situations that are presenting difficulty.
   - Comic Strip Conversations and Social Review often result in the identification of social story topics.
   - Topics may be based in misunderstandings or misconceptions an adolescent with autism has regarding a specific situation.

2. **Carefully observe the situation.**
   - Identify factors not readily observed, including variations and potential changes in routine.

3. **Write each story twice.**
   - A rough draft is written by a parent, peer, or professional.
   - The final draft is the result of input from the adolescent with autism and other relevant persons.

4. **Write with respect for the adolescent with autism.**
   - The adolescent's perspective determines the focus of a social story.
   - Never discredit the adolescent's perspective as "wrong" or "inaccurate."

5. **Follow the formula of 3–6 descriptive, perspective, or control sentences for every directive sentence.**
   - Descriptive sentences describe the situation, objectively defining where a situation occurs, who is involved, and what they are doing.
   - Perspective sentences describe the perspective of others.
   - Directive sentences describe expected responses.
   - Control sentences are written by the adolescent with autism, identifying simple strategies to use to recall information in a social story.

6. **Write according to guidelines based on the learning style of persons with autism.**
   - Individualize for an adolescent's reading ability and interests.
   - Write in the first person.
   - Avoid words or phrases that may be misleading if interpreted literally.
   - Incorporate the ideas of the adolescent with autism and others in the final draft of a story.

FIGURE 5.10. Writing social stories for adolescents with autism.

it may be effective to omit directive sentences in rough draft of a story, involving the adolescent with autism in writing directive or control sentences to include in the final draft.

Guidelines for Writing for Persons with Autism

A social story is written according to guidelines that are based on the learning characteristics of persons with autism. Each social story is individualized for ability and interests. For example, an adolescent's interests and reading and comprehension level have a significant impact on how a story is written. If a high school student with autism loves to read textbooks and easily comprehends information presented in this way, a social story may be written following a structured textbook format. If an adolescent with autism has limited reading ability, enlarged print, symbols, simple illustrations, or an audiotape may be incorporated with a story. In this way social stories consider and accommodate the ability of the reader.

Social stories are written in the first person, using that perspective to describe social skills or past, present, or future situations. For this reason, it is important to avoid statements that may inaccurately describe the perspective of the person with autism—for example, "There's no need to be afraid of . . ." or "I always have fun at parties" or "I will love gym class." Perspective sentences can be used to cover those concepts—for example, "Some people are afraid of . . . " or "Many people have fun at parties" or "Some students love gym class."

Considering the tendency of persons with autism to interpret information literally, social stories are proofread for words that could be confusing if interpreted literally. In addition, the concept of *always* may be implied unless terms like *usually* and *sometimes* are used to accurately define the frequency with which something occurs. The same is true of the concept of *everything*, which makes it important to be very specific when writing for persons with autism.

The ideas of others are incorporated prior to arriving at a final draft of a social story. The adolescent with autism reviews the rough draft. This review enables the adolescent with autism and the parent, professional, or peer to work together to check for comprehension, write control sentences, or rewrite the story to clarify information. In addition, the adolescent with autism is involved in identifying and asking relevant individuals to review and revise the rough draft of a social story. This final review catches inaccuracies, increases relevant details, and incorporates the ideas of others who are critical to the success of the individual with autism.

Though they may require assistance to learn how to use a story, adolescents with autism are given control of a social story as soon as possible. The adolescent assists in distributing final copies of the story to people who reviewed the rough draft and other people who may be impacted by the story. While a review schedule for the story may be suggested, the adolescent with autism makes the decision regarding how frequently a story is reviewed. Several stories may be placed in a notebook, enabling the adolescent with autism to independently review social information covering a variety of skills and situations as needed.

A Case Example Using a Social Story

The following case example illustrates how a social story was written and implemented with David, a high school student with autism. David is enrolled in the school choir, and a concert is scheduled in two weeks. The music teacher indicates that David has difficulty controlling his volume when he sings, requiring frequent reminders to bring his volume down.

The consultant for students with autism writes a social story to assist David in monitoring his volume. To do this, the abstract term *volume* is clearly defined using a variety of functional cues—for example, "I will sing so I can hear the people singing around me." A rough draft of the story is distributed. The music teacher asks that the story also include the use of an invisible volume control dial to indicate the need for reduced volume. The story in Figure 5.11 is the final draft of David's social story. It provides David with information he needs in order to control and monitor his own volume.

David is introduced to the story by a consultant who explains that the story has information that may be helpful to him. A copy of the final draft of the story is shared with David's music teacher and special education teacher. Initially, David is asked to read the story each day prior to choir. After reading the story one time, David's volume in choir is markedly improved. It is discovered that to maintain that success, David has to review the story each day before choir class. Gradually David gains independence in controlling his volume. At this point, the story is left in the special education classroom in a notebook containing all of David's social stories. David knows when he needs to review the story. David sings successfully with the choir the evening of the concert and independently refers to the story as needed throughout the remainder of the school year.

Summary of Social Stories

Social stories provide adolescents with autism with individualized and relevant information regarding the increasingly complex social situations they encounter. There are two drafts for

---

The Volume Story

I go to music class second hour. Mr. Talsma is my teacher. We sing songs in music. Mr. Talsma tells the choir when to start singing.

Sometimes, when everyone should start singing, Mr. Talsma says, "Ready, GO!" That's the cue to start singing sometimes.

Sometimes Mr. Talsma wants just one section to sing. He will stand close to that group of young men.

One thing is VERY IMPORTANT in music. It is important that students sing right. It is important to sing at the right volume. VOLUME is a word that means how loud someone sings. If one person sings with more volume than the rest of the choir, the choir will not sound right. One person should never sing louder than the rest of the choir without permission.

When people listen to a choir, they want to hear all the voices together. Most of the time, it is not fun to hear a choir when one person is accidentally singing louder than everyone else.

Sometimes, one person in the choir sings a SOLO. That means, they sing alone. You can tell when it's time for a solo when you are handed the microphone. If you do not have the microphone, it is not time for a solo.

A good way to sing with the right volume is to make sure you can hear the person singing next to you. People in the choir concentrate hard to do this by themselves.

It is important to sing with the right volume without being told. Students should sing with the right volume by themselves.

It is important to watch Mr. Talsma. Mr. Talsma moves his hands to tell each student in the choir what to do.

Sometimes, Mr. Talsma will ask the choir to IMITATE him. He will sing something and the students will listen. Then the students in the choir will sing what Mr. Talsma sang. Students should imitate Mr. Talsma when he wants them to. Students should not imitate Mr. Talsma at other times.

Mr. Talsma is proud when the choir sounds great. Mr. Talsma is happy when students sing with the right volume all by themselves.

FIGURE 5.11. Social story to assist an adolescent with autism with controlling his volume in a high school choir.

every social story: the rough draft and the final draft. While the rough draft is often written by one person, developing the final draft involves the review and suggestions of several people. Social stories are comprised of four different kinds of sentences: *descriptive, perspective, directive,* and *control sentences.* Several guidelines based on the learning characteristics of individuals with autism assist in writing effective social stories. Adolescents with autism have control of social stories and may determine how frequently they are reviewed. Social stories may be kept in a notebook as an ever-expanding social resource for adolescents with autism.

CHAPTER SUMMARY

Successful social interactions are based on efforts to consider and accommodate individual differences and abilities. The three social interventions described in this chapter—Comic Strip Conversations, Social Review, and Social Stories—are based on this fundamental principle. Recognizing that adolescents with autism have unique perceptions of social situations, it is critical to assist them with understanding and to provide accurate social information.

The concept of social assistance provides a common foundation for all three interventions. Social assistance is comprised of three components: (1) improving the understanding that parents, professionals, and peers have of adolescents with autism; (2) providing accurate social information to help adolescents predict, understand, and "read" social situations more effectively; and (3) help in identifying new, more effective responses to social situations.

The three social interventions described in this chapter give functional application to the concept of social assistance. Comic Strip Conversations and Social Review visually structure discussions regarding problem situations and assist the adolescent with autism in the expression of ideas and the identification of solutions to social problems. In addition, both interventions provide parents, peers, and professionals with valuable insights into the perspective of the adolescent with autism. Social stories are

short stories written with consideration of the learning style of persons with autism. These stories provide adolescents with autism with accurate social information in a way that is easily comprehended and used in social situations. Through the combined use of these interventions, the social needs of adolescents with autism are considered and accommodations are made to help improve their social understanding and develop skills to improve social participation.

REFERENCES

Covey, S. (1989). *The seven habits of highly effective people.* New York: Simon and Schuster.

Grandin, T. (1992). An inside view of autism. In E. Schopler & G. Mesibov (Eds.), *High-functioning individuals with autism.* (pp. 105–126). New York: Plenum.

Gray, C. (1992). *The curriculum system.* Publication of the Jenison Public Schools, Jenison, Michigan.

Gray, C., & Garand, J. (1993). Social stories: Improving responses of students with autism with accurate social information. *Focus on Autistic Behavior, 8,* 1–10.

Gray, C., Dutkiewicz, M., Fleck, C., Moore, L., Cain, S. L., Lindrup, A., Broek, E., Gray, J., & Gray, B. (Eds.). (1993). *The social story book.* Publication of the Jenison Public Schools, Michigan.

Gray, C. (1994). *Comic strip conversations.* Publication of the Jenison Public Schools, Jenison, Michigan.

Hobson, R. P. (1992). Social perception in high level autism. In E. Schopler & G. Mesibov (Eds.), *High-functioning individuals with autism* (pp. 154–184). New York: Plenum.

Odor, S., & Watts, E. (1991). Reducing teacher prompts in peer-mediated interventions for young children with autism. *Journal of Special Education, 25,* 26–43.

Quill, K. (1991). *Teaching children with autism and pervasive developmental disorders using visual aids* (Videotape). Manchester, MA: The Autism Institute.

Quill, K. (1992). Enhancing pragmatic development in verbal students with autism: Principles of adult student interaction. Presentation at the 1992 Annual Conference of the Autism Society of America. *Autism Society of America Conference Proceedings,* 89–90.

Twachtman, D. (1992). Sense making: Merging the wisdom of pragmatic with literacy-rich new ideas. Presentation at the 1992 Annual Conference of the Autism Society of America.

Autism Society of America Conference Proceedings, 100–101.

Wycoff, J. (1991). *Mindmapping: Your personal guide to exploring creativity and problem-solving.* New York: Berkley.

Resources

ORGANIZATIONS AND NEWSLETTERS

Autism International Network (ANI)

A self-advocacy organization of higher function-ing persons with autism.

> A.N.I.
> *Our Voice: The Newsletter of the*
>   *Autism International Network*
> Jim Sinclair, Editor
> P.O. Box 1545
> Lawrence, Kansas 66044
>
> Cost: $15.00 per year

Autism Research Institute

A nonprofit international center for dissemina-tion of research and other information to fami-lies and professionals.

> B. Rimland, Editor
> *Autism Research Review*
>   *International* (newsletter)
> Autism Research Institute
> 4182 Adams Avenue
> San Diego, California 92116

Autism Society of America (ASA)

A national organization of families and profes-sionals.

> *The Advocate: Newsletter of the*
>   *Autism Society of America*
> 8601 Georgia Avenue, Suite 503
> Silver Spring, Maryland 20910

Carol Gray/The Morning News

Carol Gray publishes a newsletter and several curricula materials through Jenison Public Schools.

> Newsletter: *The Morning News*

Curricula and Materials:

- *The Social Story Book* (1993, 1994)
- *The Curriculum System: Success as an Educational Outcome* (1992)
- *The Social Story Kit and Sample Social Stories* (1993)
- *Comic Strip Conversations* (1994)

> Carol Gray/The Morning News
> 2140 Bauer Road
> Jenison, Michigan 49428
> Phone: (616) 457-8955
> Fax: (616) 457-4070

Division TEACCH

A center for research, training, consultation, and diagnostic services for persons with autism.

> Eric Schopler, Ph.D., Director
> Division TEACCH Administration
>   and Research
> CB 7180, 310 Medical School Wing E
> The University of North Carolina
>   at Chapel Hill
> Chapel Hill, North Carolina 27599-7180
>   or
> Gary B. Mesibov, Ph.D., Codirector
> Division TEACCH Administration
>   and Research

More Advanced Autistic People (MAAP)

A quarterly newsletter for families and persons with autism.

The MAAP
c/o Susan J. Moreno, Editor
P.O. Box 524
Crown Point, Indiana 46307

Cost: $8.00 per year

Make checks payable to: MAAP Services

RELAXATION TECHNIQUES

Cautela, J. R., & Groden, J. (1978). *Relaxation: A comprehensive manual for adults, children, and children with special needs.* Champaign, IL: Research Press.

Groden, J., Cautela, J. R., & Groden, G. (1989). *Breaking the barriers: The use of relaxation for people with special needs* [Videotape]. Champaign, IL: Research Press.

Groden, J., Cautela, J. R., & Groden, G. (1991). *Breaking the barriers II: Imagery procedures for people with special needs* [Videotape]. Champaign, IL: Research Press.

A FEW BOOKS

Grandin, T., & Scariano, M. M. (1986). *Emergence labeled autistic.* Novato, CA: Arena.

McDonnell, P. (1993). Paul's story (afterword). In J. McDonnell, *News from the border: A mother's memoir of her autistic son* (pp. 327–376). New York: Ticknor & Fields.

McKean, T. (1994). *Soon will come the light.* Arlington, TX: Future Education.

Moreno, S. J. (1991). *High-functioning individuals with autism: Advice and information for parents and others who care.* Crown Point, IN: MAAP Services.

Quill, K. A. (1995). *Teaching children with autism: Strategies to enhance communication and socialization.* New York: Delmar.

Schopler, E., & Mesibov, G.B. (1992). *High-functioning individuals with autism.* New York: Plenum.

Stehli, A. (1991). *The sound of a miracle.* New York: Bantam Doubleday Dell.

Williams, D. (1992). *Nobody nowhere: The extraordinary autobiography of an autistic.* New York: Avon.

Williams, D. (1994). *Somebody somewhere: Breaking free from the world of autism.* New York: Avon.

Index